USAF
FIGHTER INTERCEPTOR
SQUADRONS

USAF
FIGHTER INTERCEPTOR
SQUADRONS

Peter R Foster

First published in Great Britain in 1994
by Osprey, an imprint of Reed Consumer
Books Limited
Michelin House, 81 Fulham Road,
London SW3 6RB
and Auckland, Melbourne, Singapore and
Toronto

ISBN 1 855324350

Edited by Tony Holmes
Page design by Paul Kime
Produced by Mandarin Offset
Printed and bound in Hong Kong

Front cover Afterburner fully kicked in and glowing, a pristine F-106A of the 101st FIS, Massachusetts ANG, departs Tyndall

Back cover Proudly wearing the Air Defense Weapons Center's crest and distinctive 'stars and bars' on its fin, this elderly F-101B sits quietly awaiting its next training sortie

Title page Hidden behind the nose cone of this F-15C Eagle is the Hughes AN/APG-63 radar, the information from which is distributed to the pilot via the AVQ-20 head-up display (HUD). These systems, the all-round vision afforded the pilot from the cockpit and a thrust-to-weight ratio of greater than one-to-one make this aeroplane the finest interceptor in the West today. In fact it goes much further than that as the battle-seasoned F-15 has proven itself in combat on many occasions, the aircraft's ability as a fighting machine being matched by the skill of its crews

Overleaf Although a jack of all trades, the F-4 Phantom II saw very limited use as a pure interceptor. A number of frontline squadrons were tasked with this demanding mission as a primary role, but unlike other jets to be given this prestigious responsibility, the Phantom II retained a secondary 'mud moving' capability. Aerospace Defense Command (ADC), which held the commitment to NORAD, converted only a few of its squadrons to the venerable F-4. However, by this fact alone it holds a place in the story. 63-7408, seen here preserved at Tyndall AFB in an uninteresting all-grey protective scheme, was the second production Phantom II built for the USAF. As such, it did not see frontline service, spending its entire career either with the Aerospace Development Test Centre (ADTC) at Eglin AFB, or the Air Force Flight Test Centre (AFFTC) at Edwards AFB

For a catalogue of all books published by Osprey Aerospace
please write to:

**The Marketing Department, Reed Consumer Books,
3rd Floor, Michelin House, 81 Fulham Road, London SW3 6RB**

Above Once the 'Topgun' in its own right, the F-106 Delta Dart policed the shores of NORAD regions in a period when the manned threat had been considered a thing of the past. Today, old lessons have had to be learnt. The 'Dart', whilst never actually achieving its conceived role in the period of the Cold War, found, in an afterlife, a short but challenging task in ensuring its successors were capable of meeting the threat. F-106B 59-0152 spent the latter part of its operational career with the 318th FIS at McChord AFB, followed by a short period with the 87th FIS at K I Sawyer. Following retirement it resided in the desert boneyard at Davis-Monthan, with an ignominious park code identity of 'FN087'. However, following the two successful drone programmes involving its Century Series predecessors, the jet was contracted to Flight Systems Inc in early 1986, and used as the pattern QF-106 airframe, receiving the identity code of AD101 in the process

Introduction

The dawning of the Cold War, and the creation of strategic bombers with a nuclear capability, were uppermost in defence planners minds during the period of the arms race of the 1950s, 60s and 70s. Defence of the Continent of the United States (CONUS) was given a priority matched only by the nation's ability to strike back, and this led to a succession of interceptor designs that were to follow on from the F-86 Sabre of the immediate post-World War 2 and Korean War periods.

The previously unpublished photographs featured in this volume describe the ultimate phase in the evolution of the USAF interceptor fighter, and concentrate primarily on the last 20 years of the breed when the defence of the United States passed from second to fourth generation aircraft.

Aerospace Defense Command (ADCOM) was charged with the all important task of protecting the homeland, and received not only the best designs but also the top aircrew in a task which turned out to be one of pure deterrence value. Its role encompassed an impressive 25-year period, during which the command's professional stance was matched by its esprit de corps — this feeling of pride in one's job was retained until ADCOM's demise in 1979.

The absorbing of the command within the structure of the Tactical Air Command (TAC) to create ADTAC was just the first step following the ending of US involvement in the Vietnam conflict. It had become clear during that period that the role of the interceptor was changing, as was that of the air force as a whole — the air force needed to work as an integrated package rather than as a mass of separate units.

The collapse of communism in Eastern Europe and the re-unification of the two Germanys reduced the threat to the United States even further, which, together with a number of arms limitation agreements, has been seen in a number of quarters as the key to a reduction in defence spending, and ultimately cuts in the requirement for specialised units to maintain a round-the-clock vigil.

As the threat has significantly reduced, so has the number of units that can be called upon to react accordingly. Equally, with the advances in technology and the concept of air power having progressed, the need for the dedicated interceptor has perhaps passed. It is noticeable that only one of the original ADCOM units is still retained within the current USAF structure (the 57th FS in Iceland), and that is an out-of-theatre unit.

The defence of CONUS passed directly into the hands of the Air National Guard some four years ago following the inactivation of the final US-based ADCOM unit, the 48th FIS, but even today this is under threat, with current thinking having the role passing back to the regular air force.

With the dedicated interceptor shortly to pass into history, I hope the photographs and information contained within this book will act as a testament to their importance in a period of world instability. Through necessity I have included a few shots of non ADCOM units simply to emphasise that they were not alone in the air defence business.

The photographs themselves are predominantly mine, taken with Nikon equipment and utilising Kodak film. I do, however, need to offer thanks to a number of individuals who have, over the years, provided me with assistance, in particular Lindsay Peacock, Don Jay and Jerry Geer.

Peter Foster
Brampton 1994

Contents

Delta Defenders

USAF interceptors had, by tradition, been gun platforms until the advent of the Century Series fighters. In fact, although we talk of 'weapon systems' as a matter of course today, in the late 1940s and early 50s, no such thing existed. The F-102 Delta Dagger was the first system to be designed from the drawing board up, and as such was to revolutionise the concept of the interceptor. Like so many of the post World War 2 era aircraft, this breed of fighting jet benefited from the innovative axis war machine inherited by the West, and the 'delta' shape so synonymous with the Convair team was in reality an improvement on the ideas conceived by Dr Alex Lippisch, and used in particular in the Me 163 Komet.

The USAF viewed the problem as one of stopping the long range bomber, which in all probability would be carrying a nuclear weapon. As such, this philosophy generated the need for a speedy solution which would involve not only designing an aeroplane capable of operating supersonically, but also equipping the finished jet with a weapons system that would operate in the same envelope. As neither existed, the USAF called for an experimental version of the ultimate product.

Time was, however, not on the side of the designers, with the air force requiring an in-service date of 1954. Forced to come up with the production article at the first attempt from the signing of the contract for two prototypes in December 1951, the company flew its first example on 24 October 1953, an achievement not far short of a miracle.

Although loosely based around the XF-92A technology research aircraft, the initial YF-102, 52-7994, was some 25 per cent larger and powered by the performance engine of the period, the Pratt & Whitney J57. Unfortunately, the jet was lost on its seventh flight following a flame-out, but during its short test career many of the early troubles with the design were identified – despite the second prototype having joined the flight programme by this stage, the problems were still defying rectification.

The major fault with the YF-102 centred around the type's inability to exceed Mach 1. In theory it was well within the design concept, but in practice the Convair engineers just could not achieve it. However, as the

Right One of the last aircraft built in 1954, 41405 was an early candidate for retirement, and it duly found itself a permanent resting place in the then SAC museum at Offutt AFB, Nebraska. The final two airframes in the 1954 production block were not so lucky, both being incorporated into the *Pave Deuce* programme as the 52nd and 61st PQM-102s coverted at the Sperry facility

aircraft had been designed without the benefits of a supersonic wind tunnel, or the results of tests carried out at the NACA Langley facility, it was decided to make use of the radical new area rule theory, which led to the so called 'coke-bottle' fuselage.

YF-102A 53-1787 was therefore produced in an amazing 117-day cycle of round-the-clock production at the company's San Diego plant. This version was some 16 feet longer than the original prototype, incorporated a coke-bottle shaped fuselage, a drooped nose and a different canopy. Installation of the up-rated J57-P41 engine delivering 15,500 lbs of thrust, saw the aircraft achieve Mach 1.2 on it maiden flight on 20 December 1954, and the following month a climb to over 55,000 feet gave further encouragement to the design team.

Although a number of other problems were identified these were relatively easily dealt with, although many modifications had to be retrofitted to aircraft already on the production line. The biggest design change centred around an enlarged fin to give better directional stability. This became standard on the 66th airframe, with most others being retrofitted. In fact the final design alteration did not occur until April 1957, by which time over half the 873 F-102s had been manufactured.

Running in parallel to the airframe design was that of the weapons system. As with most aircraft of this period, the weapons system was missile dominated, the USAF taking the view that the close air threat had ceased to exist. This thinking was to outweigh the argument for gun retention until the lessons of the past were relearnt during the Vietnam conflict. The 'Deuce' was armed with three AIM-4A radar-guided and three AIM-4C infra-red homing AAMs, all carried internally in the belly of the aeroplane. Service introduction commenced in June 1956, some way behind the initial requirement, and saw the 327th FIS, with its distinctive red and white lightning bolt tail, commissioned on the type at George AFB.

At its peak some four years later, 25 Aerospace Defense Command squadrons were flying the 'Deuce', and during its service life 102 different units utilised the Convair interceptor – a small number also found employment with the Greek and Turkish air forces

During the South-East Asian (SEA) conflict, the F-102A was one of the first frontline USAF types deployed, and although it served for a long period in-theatre it saw very little action. Even so, several aircraft were lost either over North Vietnam – 53373 on 15/12/65, 61166 on 3/2/68 and 61389 on 14/12/66 – or to Viet Cong attacks on airfields – 53371 and 61161 at Da Nang on 1/7/65 and 61165 at Bien Hoa on 12/5/67. The initial deployment saw aircraft from the 82nd and 509th FISs sent to Da Nang in 1964, before moving to Tan Son Nhut, where they operated in their normal ADC grey scheme. As time went by, however, many aircraft adopted the standard SEA camouflage, including those operated by the 509th FIS who also

Above right MASDC was the resting place for 400 or so F-102s, most of which sported Air National Guard markings. Aircraft 57-0868 wears the distinctive black tail of the 146th FIS of the Pennsylvania ANG, whilst in the background can be seen a camouflaged example (a scheme retained following a South-East Asian deployment) as well as jets displaying Louisiana ANG and 57th FIS markings; the latter unit had retired its aircraft to Davis-Monthan in 1973 following 11 years of use

Right Amid a host of tails, ten to be precise, sits F-102A 57-0824 in the markings of the 'Green Mountain Boys' from the 134th FIS Vermont ANG. The jet had only recently arrived at MASDC when this photographs was taken in May 1974, and it sports the park code 4FJ262. Over 200 were to be converted into drones, whilst many of the early arrivals were used as targets by the US Army Ballistics Establishment, located at the New Mexico Institute of Mining and Technology in Socorro

Above F-102A 53-1801 from the first production batch, seen residing in the boneyard at Davis-Monthan AFB in October 1975. At least ten airframes from this batch were retired to MASDC, with a further three finding preservation at Fresno, Boise and Lackland. None of this initial production batch were converted under the *Pave Deuce* programme, although this example served well into the 1970s with the 124th FIS Idaho ANG. In fact the Boise-based unit was one of the last to operate the 'Deuce', transitioning to the RF-4C Phantom II during the fall of 1975. 31801 had previously seen service in Europe with the 496th FIS at Hahn AFB, having been transferred from the 37th FIS in late 1959

Right The twin-seat TF-102A version of the Delta Dagger was interesting in that it had a side-by-side rather than a tandem configuration. Also, the vast frontal area caused all kinds of new aerodynamic problems resulting in a year's delay in performance testing following its first flight in October 1955. The aircraft was subsonic because of its modified cockpit area, but proved to be an ideal training platform, especially from the communication point of view. This example, 56-2359, is in the markings of the 4780th ADW from Perrin AFB, Texas, and was photographed at Davis-Monthan in May 1974

received the code 'PK' when stationed at Udorn AB, Thailand, during 1969. These particular aircraft deployed from their home base at Clark AB in the Philippines as part of programme *Candy Machine*, which provided air defence cover for South Vietnam. The 82nd FIS had deployed originally to Naha AB, Okinawa, from their home base of Travis, and were the first 'Deuces' to use in-flight refuelling. The unit returned to Naha and eventually disbanded, with the aircraft being disposed of in situ.

Post-Vietnam, the F-102s were relegated to the Air National Guard (ANG), although the design potential had been well recognised and had by this time ultimately led to its big brother, the F-106 Delta Dart. ANG employment accounted for much of the type's service use, although by 1974 it was very much on the wain. Most surviving aircraft had been retired to MASDC at Davis-Monthan AFB, with only six squadrons remaining operational — all F-102s had been sent to Arizona by 1975. Of the 873 airframes produced, some 400 examples were to be retired to Davis-Monthan. Many of these jets found further employment within the USAF's drone programme at a later date.

Delta Dart

The F-106 Delta Dart grew out of an extension of the F-102 programme, and in its early design stages was designated the F-102B. However, as the many design problems that had been associated with the 'Deuce' multiplied, the two designs separated, especially as development of the F-102B was held back by delays in the production of both the Wright J67 powerplant and the Hughes MX-1179 (later M-1) fire-control system.

The project came close to cancellation at one stage, and had it not been for the drive and enthusiasm of the Convair team, the ultimate interceptor may never have come to fruition. The prototype took to the skies for the first time on 26 December 1956, powered by the Pratt & Whitney J75 engine (the ill-fated J67 having by this stage been dropped), but the aircraft still lacked most of the MA-1 fire-control system. With the majority of the 2800-lb package missing, the one thing the aeroplane did not lack was performance, and it attained an altitude of 57,000 ft, with a speed of Mach 1.9.

Later in life, on 15 December 1959, a Delta Dart flown by Maj Joseph W Rogers set up an official world absolute speed record of 1525.95 mph (2455.736 kmh) at Edwards AFB. During 1960 Maj Frank Forsythe flew a production F-106A on a completely automatic flight from Edwards AFB, California, to Jacksonville, Florida, without in-flight refuelling.

A further two years passed from the first flight date until the F-106A finally entered service, by which time the MA-1 fire-control system was fully integrated with the Semi Automatic Ground Environment (SAGE)

Above right The ultimate interceptor. This F-106A Delta Dart was caught banking gently over the eastern seaboard of the United States on a mission from its base at Atlantic City, New Jersey. From this angle the aircraft's very clean lines are immediately obvious, whilst the big delta shape gave the jet very good handling qualities. It is also clear to see its family lineage, although the F-106 was quite obviously vastly different from its smaller Delta Dagger cousin

Right In planform the large delta shape of the F-106 wing comes to the fore, this design concept going a long way to giving the interceptor its impressive thrust-to-weight ratio from the single Pratt & Whitney J75-P-17 engine. This powerplant developed some 24,500 lbs of wet thrust against an empty airframe weight of 24,155 lbs, thus making the aircraft ideally suited to air combat

direction centres built as part of the new air-defence network. SAGE fed the MA-1, via a data link, target information such as altitude, speed, bearing and range, which kept the aircraft in silent communication with the GCI controller, necessitating input from the pilot only when target lock-on was achieved. The MA-1 was capable of selecting the intercept steering geometry and the automatic or manual attack modes either automatically, or on the pilot's command. If the SAGE system was inoperative, the pilot could utilise the airborne computer with only basic voice vectoring information. In 1958 this system was the ultimate in automated air defence, but by the early 1980s both it and the F-106 were getting somewhat long in the tooth, even though the jet itself was still a mean performer in its own right.

The last of the accepted Century Series fighters produced by Convair, some 277 single-seat F-106As and 63 twin-seat F-106Bs were built over a three-year period up to 29 December 1960. However, despite the production run being limited by US standards, technology updates were such at that time that the different batches were to see no less than 130 changes to bring all the aircraft up to the same spec!

Above Built to operate against the manned bomber in a missile engagement scenario through a data link system, rather than as a dogfighter, the aircraft boasted a cockpit that lacked clear forward vision. However, the MA-1 fire-control system did alleviate much of the pilot's workload, which meant that he did not have to visually acquire his target

Above The 119th FIS were the final operators of the Delta Dart, retiring the type in favour of the F-16 Fighting Falcon in July 1988. The last 'alert' state drawn by the unit finished on 7 July, and the 'Dart Out' ceremony was held on the 11th, ending 29 years of operational use by the last of the Century Series fighters. Here, F-106A 59-0031 is caught in a landing mode, clearly showing the high angle of attack typical of the delta-winged aircraft

The first of several programmes initiated to standardise the fleet was instigated in 1960 under the project name *Wild Goose*. A further long running project named *Broad Jump* saw, amongst other things, the installation of an IR search/track sight immediately ahead of the windscreen, whilst running concurrently with this was project *Dart Board*, which introduced a new ejector seat, fuel transfer modifications to arrest the problem of engine flame-outs and a thermal flash hood for the pilot.

A Simplified Logistics and Improved Maintenance (SLIM) programme was introduced in 1967 covering some 250 F-106 airframes. Improvements were made to the radar, DC electrical systems and automatic flight controls, whilst a further package known as project *Sixshooter* gave the 'Dart' better ECCM and a new RHAW receiver, along with a clearer blown canopy. The most significant and perhaps far reaching programme was to be the introduction of the gun.

To date, akin to the F-101 and F-102, the F-106 had been limited to missile engagement only, with the aircraft being capable of carrying a mixture of AIM-4E or F Super Falcon semi-active radar guided AAMs, AIM-4G IR guided AAMs, or the AIR-2G Genie unguided rocket with a 1.5 kiloton

Above Five Montana tails in descending serial order on the ramp at Tyndall AFB during the 1982 *William Tell* air defence weapons competition. The team were competing against Californian Darts as well as both the 49th and 318th FIS from the regular air force, but failed to take any of the honours on this occasion. This was the fourth visit by the 186th FIS to the meet, the others taking place in 1974, 1976 and 1980. The first two occasions saw the team take first place in the F-106 competition, and score more points than any other Delta Dart team in the remaining open categories

Right 1982 was the last great Century Series meet for the *William Tell* venue. In this shot, taken from the top of one of the hangars adjoining the flightline, 24 F-106s, six CF-101B Voodoos, eight F-4 Phantom IIs, 15 F-15 Eagles and five T-33As can be seen. 1984 was to be the last event in which the F-106 participated, the type being represented by the 177th FIG New Jersey ANG, 102nd FIW Massachusetts ANG and 87th FIS from K I Sawyer. In the past the ability of the 'Dart' had been recognised by the type's overall point score, but with the introduction of more formidable fire control systems as fitted in both the Phantom II and the Eagle, F-106s were quite easily pushed to the back of the pack

nuclear warhead. The introduction of a single M61A1 Vulcan 20 mm six-barrel cannon would have added a further dimension to the 'Dart's' already impressive list of abilities, and acknowledged its dogfighting capabilities. However, the programme came somewhat late in the type's career and only a very limited number of airframes were so retrofitted. Those that were modified could be identified by the tell-tale bulge in the under-fuselage which gave the six barrels room to rotate.

As stated earlier, service introduction came in May 1959 with the 498th FIS, the 'Geiger Tigers', at Spokane, Washington, who passed their F-102 Delta Daggers onto the 37th FIS at Ethan Allen AFB, Vermont. The F-106 was to remain in frontline service with Aerospace Defense Command, its successor ADTAC, and the 1st AF TAC until 1987, during which time it was capable of out performing almost any aeroplane in the US inventory. It survived a further year with the Air National Guard before the type was finally phased out by the 177th FIG, New Jersey ANG, at Atlantic City in July 1988, having completed 29 years of service.

Overseas deployment of the aeroplane had been limited initially by the lack of an in-flight refuelling capability. However, following suitable

Above F-106s always appeared in excellent condition throughout their service careers, and at a meet such as *William Tell* the crews went out of their way to ensure that everything was just perfect. On 57-2487, seen here taxying back to the main apron, the boys from 'big sky country' have made sure that no fault will be found with the unit's appearance. In spite of this, the team did not take any top honours. They were, however, runners-up in the F-106 category for the Best Weapons Control and Weapons Loading teams

Above Although a *William Tell* team boasts only five aircraft, a number of visitors usually make the trip to support their colleagues. Here, 120th FIG F-106A 57-0246 is seen on the transient apron at Tyndall AFB during the 1978 event. The unit retained the Delta Dart until 22 June 1987 when the final five aeroplanes, 57-2476, 57-2478, 57-2485, 57-2517 and 57-2530, were flown out of Great Falls to Davis-Monthan AFB for storage. This particular aeroplane had, however, been retired some months earlier, taking on the AMARC park code of 'FN128'

modification it did see some limited detachments to both Korea and Labrador in support of worldwide air defence requirements. It visited Europe only twice; once to the Paris Air Show, and as a detachment of six jets from the 5th FIS at Minot to Hahn AB in Germany during an exercise in September 1975.

Retirement saw some 159 airframes placed into storage at Davis-Monthan AFB, many of which were to be converted into drones during the third rebuild programme following similar conversions of F-102 and F-100 aircraft.

Left Part of the *William Tell* experience had been the one-upmanship and unit esprit de corps between rival outfits. Following the abolition of the ADC on 1 October 1979, and the absorption of the interceptor units into the TAC structure, such antics as special schemes and decorative artwork were very much frowned upon. However, subtle changes to schemes and ancillaries did manage to stay, witness the engine blank of this Montana F-106

Above With neat precision this pair of Montana Darts (57-2478 and 57-2464) lift off from the Tyndall runway at the start of a Profile III sortie, which was a cold mission conducted on the ACMI range against manned targets. During the 1982 *William Tell* the enemy consisted of QF-100, PQM-102B, F-106, F-4, F-15 and F-16 aircraft

Above The Aerospace Defense Weapons Center (ADWC) was responsible for not only the development of air fighting tactics and the training of air defence crews, but also providing targets for these crews to practice on. Here, an F-106B (58-0904) in the late ADWC markings taxies past two QF-100D drones (56-2912 and 56-3048), as well as F-100F proficiency trainer 56-3861, all of which were operated by the 475th WEG. This particular aeroplane became the 44th example to be retired to AMARC, having served with the same unit throughout its career

Above The penultimate 'Dart', F-106B 59-0164, seen in the avionics nose dock at Tyndall AFB in September 1978. This two-seater also spent its entire career with the ADWC, and become the 50th example to be retired to AMARC. The final operating unit of the Delta Dart at Tyndall AFB was the 2nd Fighter Weapons Squadron/325th Fighter Weapons Wing, the outfit receiving this title on 1 February 1982. When this photograph was taken the aircraft belonged to the 2nd Fighter Interceptor Training Squadron (FITS)/ADWC, which is suitably inscribed on the drop tank; the tail still sports the ADC badge

Above The first F-106 Delta Darts to be retired to AMARC came from the 48th FIS as a result of their transitioning to the F-15 Eagle. 59-0116 and 59-0122 were delivered to Davis-Monthan AFB during January 1982, followed by two more the following month. When the 325th FWW retired its aeroplanes, the total had reached over 50. In this photograph, taken in October 1988, the bulk of the aeroplanes visible are F-106Bs from Tyndall, with a 5th FIS and 49th FIS example also in evidence

Left TAC took command of ADCOM on 1 October 1979, incorporating the Air Defence Weapons Center, Fighter Interceptor Squadrons, six Air Divisions and Air Forces Iceland within its structure. Headquarters were through the Deputy Commander for Air Defense TAC, at Colorado Springs. F-106B 57-2540, seen lifting off from one of Tyndall's runways, already sports a TAC badge on the fin in place of the old ADC insignia, and a 325th FWW badge on the nose. The final *College Dart* advanced air combat training course for active duty F-106 pilots graduated at the USAF Interceptor School at Tyndall on 26 May 1983 — the pilots were from the 87th FIS

Above As a 325th FWW F-106B lands on the parallel runway at Tyndall AFB during the 1982 *William Tell* a pair of 144th FIW F-106As from Fresno, California, get airborne at the start of another competition profile. The Californian 'Darts' changed schemes after their transfer to TAC. During the 1978 meet the unit sported aircraft with bright red and white tails, with the California Republic golden bear motif in the centre. These more subdued markings were to transition across to the Phantom II when the squadron retired the 'Dart' in early 1984

Left The F-106 was an impressive performer, but in the warm climes of Florida the single J57 took up a fair length of runway to get the jet airborne. The pair of 194th FIS/144th FIW F-106As seen here were some of the first ANG aeroplanes to pass into storage. It is interesting to note that unlike the other surviving Guard units, the squadron chose to portray the TAC badge on the fin instead of the Minuteman emblem. On the starboard side the aircraft displayed the squadron badge

Above Having taken the short turning off of the runway, this 318th FIS 'Green Dragons' F-106A (59-0059) taxies back past the 2nd FWS jets that occupy the ramp adjacent to the *William Tell* area. This aeroplane was the 22nd to be retired to AMARC and had been processed by March 1984. However, it had been moved to the Flight Systems Inc base at Mojave by March 1987, becoming the fifth example to be converted into drone configuration. It returned to Tyndall in October 1988 as 'AD-105'

Left Aerodynamic braking with a delta-shaped aeroplane is very effective, although the large clamshell airbrake and the drogue parachute ensured that even on the long Tyndall runways, the Dart would stop. In fact the use of the dragchute enabled the jet to take the short turn-off adjacent to the main operating apron. This study of 194th FIS F-106A 58-0782 clearly shows the two blade aerials on the rear fuselage associated with the data-link relay, and the telltale bulge on the nose which housed the retracted 'IR' seeker head

Right All the ADC F-106 squadrons had an alert commitment away from their home base, the majority of them fulfilling this task in southern states. The only exceptions were the 49th FIS, which detached two jets as part of its NORAD commitment to Loring AFB, Maine, and the 318th FIS, depicted here, who maintained an alert commitment at Castle AFB, California, from 1 October 1981 following the inactivation of the 84th FIS. However, the unit was to operate the 'Dart' for only a further two years, with the last operational sortie being flown on 27 September 1983. 59-0147 was the 17th F-106 retired to AMARC

Above Rivalry between commands has always existed. The 48th FIS, in its ADC days, designed a badge in the shape of an F-106 containing an evil little red Jersey devil. The motto surrounding this character read 'Protectors of TAC', born out of friendly one-upmanship and slight jealousy over the F-15 Eagle that the 1st TFW had just received. By the time this photograph was taken in October 1980, the unit had become part of TAC, hence the badge on the jet's fin! I wonder if the badge described above still exists somewhere — knowing the perpetrator, the then Capt Dick Schultz, I would not be surprised if it did. Behind this jet are two other former ADC interceptors, an F-102 of the 475th WEG and a 111th FIS F-101B

Left Three former ADC F-106 users were to receive the F-15 Eagle; the 5th, 48th and 318th FISs. However, as policy changed, all three were to be inactivated and their role taken on-board by ANG squadrons. The 5th FIS was the first to lose its aeroplanes in the spring of 1988, having only begun to transition onto the F-15 on 3 December 1984. Its jets were passed to the 101st FIS Massachusetts ANG at Otis ANGB, which had begun conversion to the type when 76-0058 and 76-0128 were delivered on 15 September 1987. In October 1980, when these two Delta Darts from the unit participated in the bi-annual *William Tell* competition, they succeeded in winning both the Gen James L Price Top Gun trophy and the Top Crew Chief award

Above Ultimately, the interceptor-tasked ANG units were to receive the F-16A upon the retirement of both the F-106 and the F-4 Phantom II. One unit that transitioned directly from the 'Dart' to the Fighting Falcon was the 159th FIS, Florida ANG, located at Jacksonville International Airport. The unit was originally destined to receive the F-4D Phantom II to replace the F-106 in the early 1980s. However, when it was decided to inactivate the 87th FIS at K I Sawyer AFB, a change of policy saw those aeroplanes destined for the 159th passed on to the 179th TRS, who accepted them in place of their RF-4Cs – the unit was redesignated the 179th FIS accordingly. The Florida 'Darts' continued to maintain their commitment, including the alert at Homestead AFB, until they received their first F-16As during August 1986. The jet depicted here, 59-0060, was a relative newcomer to the squadron, having only recently been transferred in from the 84th FIS, and is seen whilst on a sortie from NAS New Orleans in September 1980

Left The 48th FIS was no stranger to Tyndall AFB as, apart from the normal detachments made by all ADC units to the Fighter Weapons School, the unit held the responsibility for the NORAD Alert. It was also the first of the NORAD units to transition to the formidable F-15, retiring its first 'Dart' during January 1982. Here, F-106A 58-0792 has cleaned up following a normal 'racy' take-off at Tyndall. This particular aircraft was transferred from the 48th FIS to the San Antonio test fleet in 1981. By October 1982 it had been passed onto the 325th FWW at Tyndall, before being finally retired to Davis-Monthan

Long Range Protector

The story of the McDonnell F-101 Voodoo is one of constant change throughout its career – conceived as a long range fighter escort; began life as a fighter bomber capable of delivering nuclear ordnance; found fame as a high speed reconnaissance platform; and became an interceptor, finally outliving most other ADC fighters in the NORAD region. Quite a tale, but one that does not really warrant closer scrutiny in this book, which is here to look at the USAF interceptor in its more recent years.

The 'One-O-Wonderful' Voodoo owes its origins to the experimental, but ill-fated, XF-88, and SAC's desire to have its outdated B-29 Superfortresses escorted on daylight bombing missions. However, as with all scenarios the changing needs often overtake planned solutions. In so far as the interceptor Voodoo was concerned, the F-101B model was both the last variant to be designed and the most prolific in number, 478 examples being produced – a number were also fitted with dual controls and referred to as the F-101F.

The F-101A made its first flight on 29 September 1954, but the twin-seat B-model did not fly until 27 March 1957, and even then it had only been put into production because of continued problems with the F-102 programme. However, such was the proliferation of technology emerging from the US aerospace industry in the 1950s that the air force could quite easily adapt one design if it was having problems with another.

Utilising the by now ubiquitous Pratt & Whitney J57 engine, the Voodoo was to be the only true Century Series fighter to have two powerplants and two crew, the former design trait giving great comfort to the men who operated the aeroplane. Like the Delta Dart, the Voodoo was linked to the SAGE system, and its weapon package consisted of the AIM-4 Falcon and

Left A pair of late production F-101B Voodoos from the 136th FIS, New York ANG, look for trade in December 1981, just months prior to the type's retirement. The unit changed its markings once ADC had been absorbed within TAC, although unlike a number of F-106 users it chose to retain the ANG Minuteman patch. The distinctive lump on the upper nose section houses the IR sensor which was added to the airframe during one of the many update programmes inflicted upon all Century Series fighters during their service careers

AIM-2A Genie AAMs. Both interception and missile control were achieved through the MG-13 fire-control system, monitored by the weapon system operator in the rear cockpit. The offensive load was made up of three AIM-4 Falcon missiles carried in a rotating weapons bay and two external hard points to accommodate two nuclear warhead Genie AAMs.

Some of the problems that had plagued the design in its early days were to remain throughout its operational career, in particular its rather off-putting tendency to 'pitch-up' without warning. However, this problem is now known to be common to all T-tailed aeroplanes, and in the Voodoo it was easily overcome providing one understood how such an unsolicited manoeuvre could be unwittingly induced. Pitch-up was caused by the wing blanking out the stabiliser when the jet was flown with a high angle of attack.

Service introduction of the F-101B came in January 1959 with the 60th FIS at Otis AFB, Massachusetts, prior to its move to L G Hanscomb Field. Its aeroplanes were all F-101B-95-MC block aircraft from the 1957 fiscal procurement, and they received the unit's attractive insignia, which consisted of three red lightning bolts on the tail surrounding the squadron's machine gun-armed black crow, on their fins. The air defence Voodoo went on to replace a number of other types in service with the ADC including the F-86L Sabre, F-89J Scorpion, F-102A Delta Dagger and F-104A Starfighter – it equipped 17 different squadrons by mid-1960. Throughout its service career some 26 units utilised to B-model Voodoo, including a number of Air National Guard squadrons.

The Voodoo interceptor had all but left the frontline inventory by the beginning of the 1970s, although its service in the air defence world was still being courted by seven ANG squadrons. Most of the frontline F-101B units had inactivated, or at least changed identities, by this stage, with perhaps the only outfit to retain its ADC role being the 84th FIS, which transitioned to the F-106A Delta Dart in September 1968 whilst stationed at Hamilton AFB, California. The swap took place at Paine Field, Washington, under the careful direction of the 498th FIS, a number of whose pilots were augmented into the unit when it returned to Hamilton AFB.

The remaining years of the Voodoo's USAF career were spent with these seven ANG squadrons and the ADWC, although their numbers began to reduce in 1972 when the 116th FIS at Spokane, Washington, became the 116th ARS and relocated to Fairchild AFB with KC-135As. They were followed by the 132nd FIS, who also transitioned onto tankers, but remained at its home base in Bangor, Maine. The other five users were more fortunate, performing in the air defence role until 1982 when they transitioned onto either C- or D-model Phantom IIs. Today, all but one of these units is equipped with the F-16, the exception being the 123rd FIS,

Above right The 136th FIS at Niagara Falls International Airport traded in its Voodoo fighters for F-4C Phantom IIs in the spring of 1982. Although equipped with of the 'One-O-Wonderful' for over a decade, the unit made only one appearance at a *William Tell* competition, and that was in 1980, the final year that the USAF included a Voodoo category within the event – the Canadians did, however, attend two years later

Right Ellington-based Texas ANG F-101B Voodoo waits patiently on the ramp at Tyndall for the start of the next day's flying. Protective covers have been applied to ensure that no moisture gets into the radar housing or the WSO's cockpit. Points could be lost through equipment malfunction, and the professionalism of these ANG ground- and aircrews made no allowances for such shortcomings. The unit, coming from the 'Lone Star' state, were very patriotic in respect of their origins, the engine blanks on this jet portraying the Texan emblem. Whilst taxying to and from the runway a Texan flag was flown on a miniature jackstaff from the rear cockpit just to confirm the unit's state of origin! During the aircraft's last *William Tell* competition, the 111th FIS took all six F-101 category trophies, as well as the overall Top Gun, Top Crew Chief and Top Avionics awards – not bad for a 23-year-old aeroplane

who traded their F-4Cs for the formidable F-15A Eagle, which it received when the 318th FIS inactivated in late 1989.

The 2nd FITS at Tyndall AFB, as part of the ADWC, had utilised the F-101B Voodoo (alongside the F-106A Delta Darts of the 95th FITS) in both the ab initio training role and as the advanced tactics and systems mount. The unit, now redesignated 325th FWW, stood the Voodoo down in early 1982, although the 82nd TATS at Tyndall AFB were responsible for the final F-101 sortie on 20 September 1982. This unit also loaned airframe 58-0300 to the Canadian Armed Forces (CAF), complete with its ECM 'hot pod'. No 414 Sqn was to be the recipient, and the ex-USAF Voodoo joined the other CF-101s within the NORAD force.

Canadian Voodoos

The Royal Canadian Air Force (RCAF), as it was then, received 56 CF-101B and 10 CF-101F Voodoos from USAF stocks during 1961 to replace its Avro CF-100 Canuck interceptors following the cancellation of the Avro CF-105 Arrow project. The aircraft were initially supplied from operational ADC squadrons, including the 84th FIS, in Operation *Queen's Row* – they were all from the final 1959 fiscal batch of F-101B-115-MC and -120-MC airframes. The crews from the 84th FIS assisted the six qualified RCAF crews in ferrying all 66 airframes to Canada.

These aircraft were assigned to five NORAD units, the first to receive the type being No 425 Sqn, then based at St Hubert, who relinquished their Canucks on 30 April 1961. The crews then undertook a systems course at Otis AFB, Massachusetts, followed by a nine-week conversion at Hamilton AFB, California. Voodoo operations, therefore, did not commence until November, when the squadron began flying from RCAF Station Namao, Edmonton, Alberta, where it remained until the following July, converting other prospective Voodoo squadrons during that period.

The units that made the transition were; No 416 Sqn in September 1961; No 410 Sqn in November 1961; No 414 Sqn in November 1961; and No 409 Sqn in March 1962. As mentioned earlier, No 425 'Alouette' Sqn moved to its present base of Bagotville, Quebec, alongside No 410 Sqn in July 1962.

Right Most *William Tell* profiles call for a four-ship engagement, F-101B 57-0370 of the 111th FIS departing on just such a sortie in October 1980. One problem facing Voodoo crews during a take-off run, especially in cold conditions, was that the rolling speed exceeded the permitted parameters for nose wheel retraction during the launch. Therefore, McDonnell designed the hydraulics to retract the forward moving nose wheel first in an attempt to overcome the problems caused by the excess thrust of the two Pratt & Whitney J57 engines

Above The 111th FIS/147th FIG retired all of their Voodoos by July 1982, having traded them in for very tired F-4C Phantom IIs, the first two of which (37650 and 40865) arrived at Ellington in March 1982. The jets came from very different backgrounds; the former had served in Vietnam, where it became a confirmed 'MiG' killer, whilst the latter was an ex-USAFE machine from the 81st TFW that had escaped transfer to Spain. Aside from the ANG facility, Ellington is home to a wide range of units including the Texas Army National Guard and a NASA facility which uses, amongst other aeroplanes, the last surviving WB-57F. Back to the F-101, this particular jet, 57-0317, sadly did not survive to enjoy its retirement in Arizona, the Voodoo being lost in a training accident on 23 October 1980 shortly after its return from the *William Tell* competition

Right The J57 engines that powered the F-101 Voodoo were hard light powerplants rather than multi-stage afterburners like today's engines. Basically this meant that vast quantities of fuel were dumped into the afterburner and ignited, rather than gradually fed in. From experience I can confirm that the kick of going into reheat was very noticeable, whilst the distinctive sound of a jet beginning its take-off run in afterburner was indicative of the era from which it came. 58-0276 from the 111th FIS was photographed just coming unstuck, and in spite of the shot being taken at a shutter speed of a 500th of a second, the background is still blurred – a fair indicator of the thrust produced by these early engines

Above The 132nd FIS/101st FIG, Maine ANG, or 'Maniacs', operated the
F-101 Voodoo from Bangor International Airport before transitioning in 1976
to more 'environmentally friendly' KC-135s that were formally with SAC. At
this stage in the Voodoo's ANG career, re-assignment was not on the cards,
however, and the jets were all retired to Davis-Monthan AFB. Unlike the
Super Sabre, 'Dagger' and 'Dart', this was one Century Series fighter that was
not to find new glory as a drone. It is assumed that the difficult handling
qualities of the F-101, and in particular its tendency to 'pitch-up', made it
unsuitable for pilotless operation. In this shot, the search light just beneath
the port side of the WSO's position is clearly visible, this device being used
for aircraft identification during air intercepts

Above Oregon (along with Massachusetts) eventually received the F-15 Eagle, thus allowing the state to retain its interceptor role. When this shot was taken in 1978, however, they were nearing the end of their time with the venerable Voodoo. Here, F-101B 58-0287 resides on the transient ramp next to a Delta Dart from the Montana ANG, whilst on the *William Tell* flightline, more F-106s from the 48th FIS sit waiting their next sortie. Overhead can be seen a pair of T-33As from the 95th FITS, which was part of the ADWC. The Voodoo's rotating weapons bay also had an arrangement whereby a luggage pack could be fitted into the space normally reserved for AIM-4 Falcon AAMs, and stored flush for flight. The luggage pack on this Voodoo is suitably inscribed to show its ownership

No 3 All-weather (Fighter) Operational Training Unit (AW(F)OTU), previously at Cold Lake and now also at Bagotville, used the CF-101 alongside its ageing CF-100s until 1964, when the OTU became an all-Voodoo operation. In March 1968 No 410 Sqn at CFB Bagotville took on the responsibility for training Voodoo crews, and No 3 AW(F)OTU deactivated.

Serialling of the Canadian Voodoos was achieved by adding the figures '17' to the final three digits of the former USAF serial. The aircraft concerned, 59-0391 to 0411, 0433 to 0453, 0455 to 0457, 0459 to 0461, 0463 and 0464, 0466 to 0472, and 0475 to 0483, became 17391 etc. Attrition in the Voodoo's early days of operation was quite high for an air defence aeroplane, with some ten aircraft being lost in the first decade of use.

By 1971 the survivors of these 66 airframes were returned to the United States in exchange for a further 66 aircraft of a higher specification. One of the things lacking on the first batch of aircraft, but incorporated in the second, was the introduction of the IR sensor on the nose, which improved the accuracy of the AIM-4D Falcon AAM.

The bulk of the aircraft returning to the US were themselves modified into a RF-101H configuration and issued to the 192nd TRS, Nevada ANG, at Reno International Airport. The 'new' arrivals for the CAF were drawn from the 1956 and 1957 fiscal F-101B procurement. However, almost coincidental with the arrival of these aircraft came a revised CAF serialling system. This saw a three-digit type serial precede a three-figure airframe serial. In the case of the Voodoo, the type serial was logically 101, whilst the aircraft were serialled 001 to 066, creating a serial 101001 etc.

By this stage No 414 Sqn had ceased Voodoo operation in favour of a CF-100/ET-133 mix. However, the four remaining units kept the Voodoo on line until 1982 when No 410 Sqn became the first of the quartet to stand down and convert onto the futuristic CF-18 Hornet. The opportunity was taken at the same time to withdraw a further six airframes, whilst the residue were distributed amongst the surviving three squadrons. The ANG was also building up to their Voodoo finale south of the border, one of the last USAF flights with the jet seeing a weary ADWC airframe from Tyndall

Left The twin-stick version of the F-101B was identifiable by the lack of an IR sensor on the nose and the absence of the searchlight in the port side housing, as on this ADWC aircraft. Operating with the 2nd FITS and being flown solo on this occasion, 70297 boasts a 'hot pod' for target duties during a non-firing phase of the competition. Behind the ejection seat in the rear cockpit can also be seen the blind flying canopy for student instrument check rides. Photographed late in the Voodoo's career (October 1980 to be exact), this jet displays a TAC badge in place of the ADC decal

passed to No 414 Sqn at CFB North Bay, who converted it into an ECM-optimised EF-101B.

At first the squadron operated this machine as a one-off in normal ADC light grey colours, adding just the unit's red and black stripes to the rudder, as well as the national insignia to the fuselage and wings. By 1984, the 'Black Knights' had repainted the jet black overall and reserialled it 101067, thus adding it to the existing serial batch.

The jet continued to operate from North Bay until 1985, by which time it had been joined on the squadron by CF-101F 101006, whose task it was to maintain crew currency. No 425 Sqn was the second to stand down in the fall of 1984, the unit transitioning to the CF-18. This was followed by No 409 Sqn at CFB Comox and finally No 416 Sqn at CFB Chatham. The 'electric jet' continued to provide valuable training during the work-ups of the CF-18 units until late 1985, when it was finally returned to the USAF. It now resides on permanent display in Minneapolis-St Paul, but in its former USAF markings. No 414 Sqn have subsequently preserved CF-101B 101057 at CFB North Bay, painted black in memory of this impressive aeroplane.

Above Canada began operating the Voodoo during 1961. Less than a decade later it had traded in the survivors of its first batch of aircraft for 66 airframes of a higher modification state. For much of its career, the CF-101 operated in natural metal, and it was only during the twilight years that a more protective overall grey scheme was adopted. However, during the 1980 *William Tell* competition the CAF composite team brought with them a single 'naked' aircraft, 101042, sporting a non-standard badge to complete the effect

Above No 425 'Alouette' Sqn, call sign 'Lark', operated from CFB Bagotville, a base located on the outskirts of Chicoutimi in central Quebec Province. Traditionally a French speaking heartland – in fact down town you would be unlikely to hear anything else – the squadron was bi-lingual in so far as aircrew were concerned, having a requirement to be proficient in both French and English. However, at the lower echelons this was not always the case, and thus it was not possible to have a completely integrated unit and all technical manuals had to be in both languages! Even the jets carried both English and French stencilling, as shown here on 101056 – this Voodoo also displays a *William Tell* marking on the rear fuselage. Despite the fact that the CF-101 has not yet finished its rotation, the WSO has already gone 'head down' over the radar scope, priming his ancient equipment in readiness for combat

Above Bagotville is located, as the crow flies, only some 160 miles from Loring AFB where the 49th FIS held its NORAD alert. As a result of this close proximity, the commitment was shared between the two units, although No 425 Sqn also maintained a 'Cold Shaft' state as well. This involved having to scramble to Gander in Newfoundland, refuel, then intercept incoming traffic and escort it south until relieved by the 49th off the eastern seaboard. These intercepts took place at extreme range usually at night, and mainly comprised Tu-95 and Tu-142 bombers transiting to Cuba. It was not unheard of for the *Bear* crews to try and deliberately lure the CF-101s further out to sea by altering their southward track – in a single manned aeroplane this could have had disastrous affects, but fortunately the two-man system allowed an accurate check on course and heading to be maintained whilst still shadowing the Soviets. The nearest jet depicted here is a CF-101F twin-sticker, identifiable not only by its serial but also the red and white striped rudder, which was a legacy of its former use by No 410 'Cougar' Sqn, the Voodoo OCU

Left CF-101s 003, 064 and 002 in formation. The two twin-stickers, 003 and 002, carry the striped rudders, with the former also sporting the remains of the red and white striped band around the wings. The upper inner wing sections were painted red, unlike the CF-101Bs which were blue. Both F-models are fitted with IR sensors on the nose, thus making them fully combat capable. No 425 'Alouettes' Sqn was the first frontline unit to stand down during late 1984 in favour of the CF-18, the OTU having already gone down that road some two years previously

Double Ugly

The Phantom II's exploits as a fighter over Vietnam during eight long years of war are legendary, the USAF crews flying the jet being credited with 122 kills and their compatriots in the Navy claiming a further 41. Both scores are worthy tributes to a magnificent aeroplane and a very efficient radar. Interestingly, most of these kills are attributed to Beyond Visual Range (BVR) missile engagements, as designers of the 1950s era believed that the gun was an obsolete weapon.

Many fighter pilots who experienced combat during the Vietnam War stated that had they had the gun then many more kills would have been achieved. Fortunately, designers took heed of these words, and both the F-4E and all postwar combat aircraft have had an internal weapon fitted as standard..

However, as much as the fighter pilot will state that the gun only comes into its own in a close air environment, they will also tell you that it is not always wise to find oneself in such a situation. Today's fighter pilot is taught to kill before being killed – that is shoot before the opposition sees you, and therefore the missile becomes the best option. Equally, the ability of the current generation of short range weapons such as the AIM-9M, with its all-aspect seeker head, perhaps to some degree supports the 1950s and 60s missile mentality. Therefore, is the gun really needed?

The Phantom II was tasked with performing the role of a pure interceptor very late on in its career with the USAF. True, a number of Tactical Fighter Wings did control F-4 squadrons that had a primary air defence tasking such as the 36th TFS within the 51st TFW (now FW) at Osan AB, Korea, and the 525th TFS/86th TFW at Ramstein AB, Germany. In fact, the former unit would probably have been horrified to have been accused of being in the mud-moving business, having shot down an estimated 315 MiG-15s whilst equipped with F-86s during the Korean War!

Right F-4D Phantom II 64-0949 of the 178th FIS/119th FIG, North Dakota ANG, nicknamed 'The Happy Hooligans', resplendent in the attractive high gloss air defence grey scheme so favoured by the ADCOM units, and adopted by the first of the Fargo jets in July 1979. The unit was the second ANG squadron to receive the Phantom II, the first, the 'HANGmen' of the 199th FIS, Hawaii ANG, becoming PACAF controlled soon after conversion and being redesignated a TFS as a result. This particular aeroplane, following its Vietnam service, became part of the 49th TFW at Holloman AFB, before being issued to the 178th

Right F-4D 64-0975 '24' of the 178th FIS never saw action in Vietnam, having been assigned to USAFE and the 36th TFW at Bitburg, before returning to the United States with the 49th TFW at Holloman, New Mexico. Seen here on the transient ramp at Tyndall AFB in October 1982, this jet displays a unit citation and ANG badge on the fin. The F-4D was retired by the unit on 16 February 1989 as later airframes became available

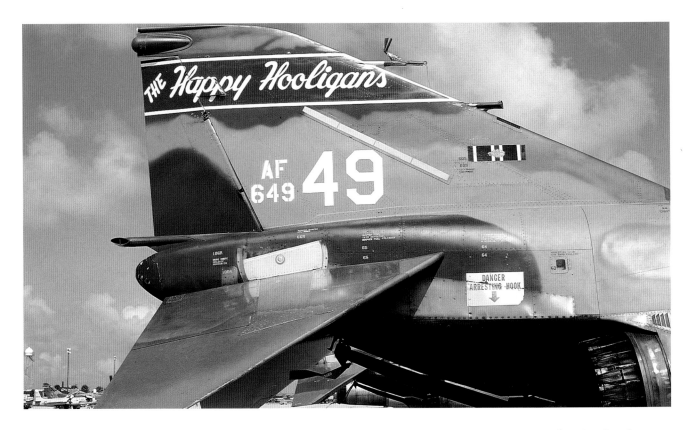

It was the demise of the Century Series fighter that brought the Phantom II into the world of ADCOM. Post-Vietnam, when force reductions were taking place and both the F-4E and F-15 were beginning to replace the older F-4C/D models, a limited programme was introduced to supply surplus airframes to the Guard. Although Phantom IIs were sent to the tactical squadrons, which retained a limited air defence role, it was also decided to replace the aging F-101 Voodoos that equipped the 178th FIS with surplus F-4Ds.

The 199th FIS 'Happy Hooligans' were to be the first ADCOM-controlled unit to receive the Phantom II, the squadron transitioning from the F-102A to the F-4C in 1974, but in the process they also switched to the tactical role. In fact the only regular ADCOM squadron that made use of the Phantom II was the 57th FIS, who received the F-4C in the early 1970s as a replacement for the Delta Dagger. ADWC began operating the type in 1977, but decided to trade in these jets two years later, thus leaving the re-equipment programme exclusively to the ANG. The D-model Phantom IIs from the first production batch began arriving at Fargo in March 1977, these jets, 64-0937, 938, 939, 942, 945, 949, 952, 953, 956, 959, 963, 965, 968, 970, 972, 973, 975,

Above 64-0949 shortly after the 178th FIS transitioned to the Phantom II.. The unit still retained the SEA tactical camouflage scheme worn by the jet when on strength with the 49th TFW. Although one of the first aircraft taken on charge at Fargo, it was also to be one of the last Phantom IIs operated by the unit. It, in company with 64-0953, 0956 and 68-949, performed the final four-ship departure on 10 April 1990 as the aircraft were ferried to Davis-Monthan AFB for storage, where they still reside today

Above One of the original ADCOM F-4C Phantom IIs was 63-7618. Assigned to the 57th FIS at Keflavik, Iceland, in October 1975, the aircraft was originally operated in the tactical camouflage scheme. It was a member of the team that participated in the 1976 *William Tell* competition, the unit sporting completely chequered tails for the event. Eighteen months later it was one of the first F-4Cs to adopt the ADCOM air defence grey scheme, before being replaced within the squadron by an F-4E

976, 977 and 979, being received predominantly from the 49th TFW at Holloman AFB. Weary airframes that had already experienced almost 15 years of frontline service, these jets were the survivors of the USAF's first Phantom II production order, the other aircraft in the batch having either been lost in combat or transferred to the Republic of Korea Air Force (RoKAF).

The choice of the Phantom II as a replacement for ADCOM assets was perhaps really decided as long ago as 1961 when it was pitted against the F-106A during Project *Highspeed,* from which the F-4 emerged as a true thoroughbred. The F-4D's radar was the part-solid state APQ-109, which was optimised for air-to-ground operations, coupled to the AN/APN-157 radar set group, the ASN-48 inertial navigation system and AGM-12 air-to-ground missile control system. This differed from the US Navy's F-4Js, which were equipped with the AWG-10 pulse-doppler with its look-down capability.

The earlier F-4C's AN/APQ-100 radar was also capable of plan position mapping, and although optimised primarily for the 'mud-moving' role, the jet boasted an optical sight as well as an AAA-4 Infrared seeker under the

Left 14 June 1978 saw 63-7618 transfer from the 57th FIS to the 171st FIS Michigan ANG at Selfridge ANGB, replacing an F-106A Delta Dart. Initially coded '15', it had become '17' by the time this shot was taken in 1982. In line with ADCOM unit tradition, the 171st adopted a scheme almost identical to the Dart, with yellow and black chequers on both the rudder and the splitter vane. Consideration was also given to the overall look of the jet, the external fuel tanks and luggage pod, for example, receiving highly polished chrome ends. None of the 171st's F-4Cs were retired to AMARC, most finding their way into ground instructional roles including Battle Damage Repair Training (BDRT) and decoy duties, although a few were transferred to other units, principally the 123rd FIS

Above In 1982 63-7618 was the pride and joy of crew chief Mike Galea, sporting the name 'Double Trouble'. Virtually all the unit's jets wore personal names by the time that year's *William Tell* competition came around. Most airframes hailed from the early 1963 production batch, many of which had been retained in the USA during the Vietnam War with training units; the frontline squadrons were issued with new-build 1964 models. However, not all of the 171st's aeroplanes were to have such an uneventful history, 63-7666, for instance, having seen action with the 557th TFS/12th TFW at Cam Ranh Bay between 1968 and 1970, prior to being issued to the 57th FIS. This particular jet was to end its days as BDRT airframe at Kunsan AB, South Korea

Above Most of the 171st FIS's Phantom IIs were to come from Iceland, and 37460 '06' 'Puff the Magic Dragon' was no exception. However, this particular airframe was one of the few to see service with the Air Defense Weapon Center during 1978, before transfer to the Michigan Guard

nose to allow limited air defence operations to be performed. Indeed, both the Air Force and Navy flew a good number of pure MiGCap missions.

The 178th FIS were the sole operators of air defence optimised Phantom IIs for approximately 12 months, the squadron being joined next by the 171st FIS Michigan ANG at Selfridge ANGB, who began receiving the C-models in May 1978. The North Dakota boys had, up to this time, been content to operate their aeroplanes in the standard South-East Asian camouflage scheme, although they were quick to add their traditional red unit band across the fin, which contained a white 'Happy Hooligans' logo, in time for their participation in the 1978 *William Tell* competition.

In 1980 both the Selfridge- and Fargo-based units were at Tyndall for the biannual meet, their jets receiving a high gloss grey colour scheme reminiscent of their former glory days, a finish which also harked back to previous Century Series mounts. These were to become probably the 'prettiest' Phantom IIs of all time; such was the spirit of that 1980 meet (the last before TAC toned things down), the 171st had their own station wagon in identical colours, complete with a Sparrow missile! Alas, this was not to last.

Even at this early stage in the life of the Phantom II, the F-15 Eagle was beginning to take hold. At the 1982 event only two F-4 teams were represented at Tyndall, despite the fact that the 57th FIS had by this time re-equipped with the F-4E model — this transition occurred in March 1978 when the frontline unit began receiving early production model aircraft from the 1966 fiscal order.

The 123rd FIS Oregon ANG at Portland IAP transitioned to the F-4C during 1982, and were ready to do battle with the longer serving Guard Phantom II squadrons by the time *William Tell 84* was staged. The 136th FIS at Niagara Falls IAP and the 111th FIS at Ellington, Texas, also transitioned during this period, with the latter unit receiving its first two jets (63-7650 and 64-0865) during March 1983. This left the Californian 'Bears', the 194th FIS, to follow suit by 1984, giving ADTAC five users of the F-4C; a further 16 Guard squadrons were to operate the variant in the tactical role.

In 1976 the Minnesota ANG had traded its F-101B Voodoo interceptors in for recce RF-4Cs, changing its role and title to the 179th TRS in the process. However, in a further change of Guard policy, the unit was to receive the D-model Phantom II during 1984, thus reverting back to its previous ADTAC role. The aircraft concerned had originally been destined to replace F-106A Delta Darts with the 159th FIS, Florida ANG. However, with ADTAC's decision to inactivate the 87th FIS at K I Sawyer AFB, the 179th FIS had to be able to take on the latter's alert commitment.

The D-model was also becoming surplus in ever increasing numbers by this time, which allowed a number of units already operating the older but basically similar F-4C to upgrade. First, it was decided that the Guard would take on its own training as the regular air force was no longer in a position to offer that service with the aeroplane being rapidly phased out. To accomplish this task the 112th TFTS was formed under the 142nd FIG at Kingsley Field, Oregon, the unit receiving C-model airframes. Next, it began to upgrade all the other users with low-hour D-models, the exception to this rule being the 123rd FIS at Portland, who retained their aging jets until late 1989.

Left This particular jet was not part of the 1982 *William Tell* competition, as the luggage pod confirms. However, 63-7622 '18' was unusual in that it was quite a late addition to its unit establishment, having transferred from the 58th TTW at Luke AFB, rather than the 57th FIS. The jet had spent its early career with the 4453rd CCTW, which ultimately became the 58th TTW, and therefore did not see action in Vietnam

Above F-4C 63-7618 early on in its service career with the 171st FIS, when it operated with the code '15'. Seen lifting off at the start of a practice intercept mission, the jet cleans up for a sortie that will probably last around 90 minutes. Despite being fitted with two external 308.5 imperial gallon fuel tanks, the F-4 may well also employ inflight refuelling if it is available. The Phantom II's primary weapon was the beyond visual range (BVR) capable AIM-7 Sparrow missile, which weighed in at around 400 lbs, with a 60 lb warhead. Some 12 ft in length, the AIM-7E variant had a range off about 14 miles — later versions, such as the AIM-7L, were significantly improved in terms of both reliability and range

Right This Phantom II was another to miss out on service in South East Asia. 63-7482 spent its early life with the 4453rd CCTW, before being transferred to the 92nd TFS/81st TFW at RAF Bentwaters under USAFE control on 28 January 1972. The jet served as a replacement for the airframes transferred to the Spanish Air Force, although by May 1974 it had moved to the 401st TFW at Torrejon in Spain, following the departure of the wing's F-4Es to the 36th TFW at Bitburg. The 171st picked the jet up from 58th TTW at Luke AFB, who had operated it during 1979/80

Whilst this transition was taking place, the Guard was called upon to take on the 'Zulu Alert' at Ramstein AFB in West Germany whilst the 86th TFW converted from the F-4E Phantom II to the F-16C Fighting Falcon. Therefore, under an exercise called *Creek Claxon*, eight F-4Ds were detached to maintain the alert status, a task they carried out for almost 13 months. The first four aircraft, 64-0963, 968, 972 from the 178th FIS, North Dakota ANG, and 65-0585 from the 179th FIS, Minnesota ANG, arrived from Andrews AFB on 1 March 1986. These were followed two days later by 65-0595 and 65-0648, also from the 179th FIS, and 65-0740 and 65-0747 from the 194th FIS, California ANG.

Following a period of familiarisation sorties and the successful completion of an Alert Force Readiness Inspection (AFRI), US Air Force Chief of Staff Gen Charles A Gabriel officially announced that the 'Zulu Alert' tasking would be an Air National Guard commitment from 7 April 1986. During this period the detachment maintained four jets on permanent alert armed with a normal complement of four AIM-7E Sparrow MRAAMs, semi-recessed into the fuselage underside, up to four AIM-9G Sidewinder SRAAMs on underwing pylons, a SUU-23 gun pod on the centre line station, and additional external fuel tanks. Live scrambles occurred, on average, two to three times a week, and crews were rotated continually from the United States over this period.

The complement of aircraft was increased by one during the year when 65-0583 was added to the detachment. However, the commitment was stood down on 31 March 1987 and the first five aeroplanes, 65-0585, 65-0595, 65-0648, 65-0740 and 65-0747 returned to the United States by way of Niagara Falls on 3 April, followed by the remaining four, 64-0963, 64-0968, 64-0972 and 65-0583 on 6 April.

Guard air defence units never operated the newer F-4E model of the Phantom II, instead receiving fourth generation hardware in the shape of either the F-15 and F-16. The reasons behind this were twofold. Firstly,

Left With a take-off weight of 53,797 lbs, this 171st FIS F-4C has just become airborne after using some 3380 ft of runway. The two General Electric J79-GE-15 engines, each creating 17,000 lbs of thrust with the afterburners selected, gave it a rate of climb of 8210 ft per minute at a military rating. The aircraft was designed to operate most effectively with a combat weight of 36,140 lbs, and perform a high altitude CAP profile in this configuration for roughly 90 minutes, with a total flight time of around 160 minutes. The unit retired its F-4Cs during 1986, after which six were flown across the Atlantic for ground instructional duties; 63-7446 arrived at Aalhorn on 17 July; 63-7453 at Soesterberg on 13 June; 63-7536 at Norvenich on 17 July; 63-7576 at Bitburg also on 17 July; and 63-6710 to Lakenheath on 16 July. All told, some 19 C-model Phantom IIs found that their final flights were one way trips to Europe

Above The 111th FIS at Ellington AFB, Texas, was another unit to trade its early F-4C Phantom IIs in for the later D-model when the 31st TFW converted to the F-16. The Texas ANG unit re-equipment programme has run along parallel lines to that of the 136th FIS since both squadrons traded in their aging F-101B Voodoos in 1982. The jet depicted here, 66-7467, had been a factory-fresh assignment for the 50th TFW at Hahn AB in Germany. It later served with the 417th TFS/49th TFW, the 474th TFW and finally the 31st TFW, before finding its way to Ellington. One of the first Phantom IIs stood down by the unit, it was sent to AMARC on 6 September 1989, becoming park code airframe FP299

Right The 136th FIS first received the F-4C Phantom II in April 1982. At that time the aircraft were sporting the normal ADCOM high gloss paint scheme with the rainbow rudder. However, during November 1986 it began to receive the F-4D version, and over the next five months nine of its earlier aeroplanes were ferried to Davis-Monthan AFB for storage. The D-models assigned to the unit came mainly from the 31st TFW at Homestead AFB, although a few examples, including 66-0259, transferred in from the 141st TFS New Jersey ANG when that unit upgraded to the F-4E. The jets gradually began adopting the new standard grey camouflage which had replaced the European One green scheme so favoured by TAC during the late 1970s and early 1980s. The 136th FIS were the last users of the F-4D Phantom II, save a few test establishments

Above F-4C 64-0777 'Menace', sporting a red star on the splitter vane commemorating its MiG kill on 20 May 1967 whilst operating with the 389th TFS/366th TFW. The kill was the first of three for Lt Col Robert F Titus (pilot) and 1st Lt Milan Zimer (Weapons System Officer), the other pair occurring two days later in 64-0776; all their victories were against MiG-21s. The latter aircraft had already destroyed a MiG-21 the month before whilst being flown by Maj Robert F Anderson (pilot) and Capt Fred D Kjer (Weapons System Officer). Titus and Zimer, as call-sign 'Elgin-03', had been part of a flight of four jets covering F-105s some 20 miles north of Hanoi when a pair of MiG-21s attacked the formation. In a high speed, mostly supersonic, fight, 40777 had been forced to break-off one engagement but had got involved in another a short time later – the MiG was only downed after three missiles had been fired as the first two AIM-7s had failed to track. The 123rd FIS at Portland was to be the final user of the venerable F-4C, and had on strength at least three 'MiG Killers'; the two jets mentioned, and 63-7683 'Wild Turkey

II', which was credited with its MiG-21 kill on 2 January 1967 whilst serving with the 'Triple Nickel', the 555th TFS/8th TFW. On that same flight the legendary Col Robin Olds claimed his second MiG

Right During the 1988 *William Tell* competition, the 474th TFW from Nellis AFB deployed to Tyndall to act as targets for the mission profiles to be flown by the meet's participants. This was the first occasion that the F-16 had operated from Tyndall as part of the competition, and was perhaps a sign of changes to come. In the past other TAC units had undertaken similar duties, although these had been Phantom II operators. In this shot F-16A 80-0484/NA of the 474th TFW is framed by the tail of 111st FIS F-4D 65-0749. This particular jet was transferred to the Ellington unit from the 127th TFTS at McConnell AFB, Kansas. It had previously seen service with three USAFE wings, the 50th, 81st and 401st. It was also one of the last two F-4s retired by the unit when, in company with 65-0655, it was flown to Davis-Monthan on 12 January 1990

Above ADWC was to be one of the shortest users of the venerable Phantom II, flying the type for approximately two years. Under ADCOM the jet was introduced to coincide with the general upgrade planned for ADC and ANG units. However, when TAC absorbed ADC on 1 October 1979 the policy changed, and the Phantom II disappeared from the structure of the 325th TTW very shortly afterwards. 63-7460, depicted here, had been received by the unit from the upgrading 57th FIS, and was in turn passed on to the 171st FIS. 63-7685 in the background followed a similar route, but was transferred to the 111th FIS by the Michigan ANG in June 1982. After five years with the ANG, the jet became one of few F-4Cs to end its days in AMARC, arriving at that location on 6 May 1987

Left In this shot there are 31 F-4C/D Phantom IIs lying in store at AMARC on the outskirts of Davis-Monthan AFB. The majority had arrived there from Air National Guard units, and included examples from Texas, New York and Oregon. Up until March 1993 some 1247 Phantom IIs of all marks had passed through AMARC's doors, the majority of which are still lying in store. Many of the US Navy F-4B/J/N/S airframes will be converted to drone configuration for the Navy, whilst the F-4E/G and RF-4Cs will appear in similar programmes for the USAF/US Army. It seems unlikely that the F-4C/D variants will find further use, although in this shot one aeroplane has been stored in a protective bag, presumably with some future use in mind

Left The only ADC unit to utilise the F-4E version of the Phantom II was the 57th FIS, who converted from C-models to less than pristine Echoes in early 1978. This example, wearing the now familiar ADC high gloss grey air defence colour scheme and sporting the 57th FIS's black and white chequered tail fin, also displays an Air Forces Iceland badge on the intake and a TAC badge on the fin. 67-0315 arrived at Keflavik from the 31st TFW at Homestead AFB, but prior to this it had served with the 3rd TFW at Clark AB. During the Vietnam conflict it operated with both the 469th TFS and 34th TFS in Thailand. Not amongst the initial batch of F-4Es delivered to the 57th, it failed to see retirement, crashing on 5 September 1986

although the USAF considered the F-4E a viable air defence option at medium level, the AN/APQ-120 was not suited to the air intercept role because it lacked a look-down/shoot-down capability. The adoption of the ASX-1 Target Identification System, Electro-Optical (TISEO) system and the ASG-26 computing sight to aid identification, did, however, create a better package in both the air defence and air to ground roles. Secondly, it was felt that the Phantom II was very much on the decline, and sufficient F-16As would soon be available to allow a straight transition of most units over a relatively short timescale. Therefore, in the interim period those few units operating the older model F-4s would have to continue to do so.

The final *William Tell* competition to include a Phantom II category was held in 1988 when the 136th FIS and 111th FIS participated with their F-4D models and the 123rd FIS with their well-worn F-4Cs. As with all Guard units, the aircraft were crewed by old heads who in the game of air defence, particularly the close air threat, can be more effective than superior equipment.

Although the heyday of ADCOM had long gone, the spirit of the meet attempted to appear. The 123rd FIS jets were all veterans of Vietnam, three of which had confirmed MiG kills, and all displayed the names they had adopted during the conflict. Unfortunately, the names were somewhat discrete, but they were to be the last offerings before the spirit of ADCOM was finally purged.

Above Drawn from the initial F-4E production batch, this aircraft was previously assigned to the 1st TFW and then the 56th TFW at McDill AFB. One of the first jets to be transferred to the 57th FIS, it served with them until at least October 1982. On 9 July 1987 it was flown to Turkey following its transfer to that air force

Left Many Tactical Fighter Wings were to have squadrons that had a primary tasking of air defence. One such unit was the 36th TFS, as part of the 51st TFW, whose heritage in air combat included a large total of MiG kills during the Korean War. Based entirely in the PACAF theatre, it was to become the very last USAF regular air force air defence Phantom II operator. The jet depicted here, 68-0329, spent over half of its operational career with that one unit, and has since been re-assigned to the RoKAF. It was photographed here lifting off from the Osan runway in October 1987, sporting the unit's shark's teeth marking and 'OS' tail code

Eagles And Falcons

Service introduction of the F-15 Eagle began in November 1974 when that most famous of USAF combat squadrons, the 555th TFS 'Triple Nickel', reformed at Luke AFB. This momentous occasion was to turn the whole air defence world upside down as the USAF now possessed an aeroplane that was not only the finest interceptor ever built, but was also capable of achieving air supremacy.

However, as far as the American interceptor was concerned, the arrival of this jet signalled a move away from the pure air defence-assigned squadron, the equivalent fighting unit now performing tactical tasks as well.

The F-15 Eagle was conceived as the result of a two-year study undertaken jointly by both the USAF and the aerospace industry to find a fighter replacement for the F-4 Phantom II in the counter air threat role. The concept called for an aircraft that was capable of meeting 'Beyond Visual Range' (BVR) interception requirements, as well as having the ability to counter close air threats.

Built around two Pratt & Whitney F100-PW-100 turbofan engines, each developing 23,820 lbs of thrust, a fire control system benefiting from the Hughes APG-63 radar and some of the finest air-to-air missiles on the market, the F-15 had to be good, but it also had to be big! By situating the two engines side by side in a shallow rear fuselage, and using twin fins, the radar cross section was drastically reduced.

The Eagle must be considered as typically American. After all, the Cadillac was big, the Boeing 747 was big and by 1950s standards even the Voodoo was big, so it perhaps comes as no surprise that the F-15 turned out the way it did. Unfortunately, when something is that big then inevitably the price tag tends to fit. This has resulted in a very limited export potential, especially to America's European partners, for as much as most

Right A pleasing line up shot of F-15A Eagles waiting on the Tyndall flightline for students on the 325th FW long course to begin another day of intensive training. In this view the pilot is allowing his systems to align before taxying out whilst the crew chief looks on. The Eagle arrived at Tyndall on 15 October 1983 for use by both the 1st and 2nd Fighter Squadrons, known at that period as TFTSs. The 95th TFTS activated on the F-15 in 1988 when the last T-33As were retired from the 325th TTW (now FW). The wing took on all Eagle air defence training from the 405th TTW at Luke AFB in 1990, the latter outfit concentrating on F-15E Strike Eagle operations

would have liked the jet, very few could have found the cash to support its purchase.

World peace was something that the presence of a high profile military had brought since the end of the Vietnam conflict. However, even here dominance by air power, albeit with restrained political will, had failed to make any difference to the final outcome. In a more 'civilised' war things would of course be different. Hopefully, such a thing in Europe will never happen, but as we all know the smallest fire can burn into an inferno.

Such a spark occurred in the Middle East in August 1990 when the forces of Saddam Hussein attacked and overran the neighbouring country of Kuwait. The significance of this would no doubt have been lost upon most of us, apart for some well meant indignation, if it had not been for the presence of the bulk of the world's oil supplies in the region.

Operation *Desert Shield*, followed by Operation *Desert Storm*, have been well documented and will be an everlasting testimony to what well planned and well co-ordinated air power can achieve. In the four-week period of *Desert Storm*, some 41 Iraqi aircraft were destroyed during 33 intercepts, and a further three jets were downed after the cease fire. Of these, all bar six of the kills were made by F-15s, which were providing most of the in-theatre CAPs — 21 engagements were achieved through BVR, or with the aid of AIM-7 Sparrow missiles.

The honour of the first confirmed kill during the conflict originally went to Capt S W Tate in F-15C 83-0017 of the 71st TFS/1st TFW. However, following detailed examination of the AWACS tapes it was discovered that Capt J K Kelt of the 58th TFS/33rd TFW in F-15C 85-0125 actually shot his MiG-29 down at 3.10 am on 17 January 1991, some 44 minutes before the Mirage F.1 credited to Capt Tate.

Desert Storm was the climax of the 20-year history of the F-15 with the USAF, the jet having earlier been used with outstanding effect by the Israeli AF/DF. Service introduction in the United States began as stated with the training unit at Luke AFB, as well as evaluation flying by the 57th FWW at Nellis AFB. The first frontline unit to work up on the Eagle was the 1st TFW at Langley AFB, which reformed on 1 July 1975 specifically for this purpose. The unit's first jet, F-15A 74-0083 arrived on 9 January 1976, and apart from transitioning to the upgraded F-15C model, the unit has retained its links with the type ever since.

Training on the F-15 was initially carried out at Luke AFB under the auspices of the 58th TTW, and later, when the introduction of the F-16 had occurred, it transferred to the 405th TTW, utilising a mix of F-15A/B/C and D airframes. Today, the base retains its association with the F-15 through the Strike Eagle variant, the air defence training commitment having been re-located to Tyndall AFB.

Above right F-15A 76-0042/TY with a yellow fin tip and stylised markings to represent the 2nd FS commander's personal mount. The jet had previously seen service with the 53rd TFS/36th TFW at Bitburg, who received it fresh from St Louis on 23 September 1977. It was later transferred to the 525th TFS in April 1978, then back to the USA when the squadron began receiving the upgraded F-15C model. In America it served initially with the 33rd TFW at Eglin AFB, before transferring to the 405th TTW at Luke. It came to Tyndall AFB when air defence training began to wind down in Arizona. In this shot, the jet is being prepared for a training mission, although it will not be a live weapon sortie as the trolley of AIM-9 Sidewinder and AIM-7 Sparrow missiles are destined for another customer

Right A red fin tip signifies an aircraft belonging to the 1st FS at Tyndall AFB. The middle jet in this shot not only displays the 325th TTW badge but also that of the 1st AF. The unit originally came under ADTAC control until the 1st AF was created in 1986. At that time it assumed command of not only the 325th TTW, as it was then, and the ADWC, but the 23rd AD at Tyndall, 24th AD at Griffiss, 25th AD at McChord, 26th AD at March, Air Forces Iceland and the 4700th ADS (DewLine)

RESCUE
EMERGENCY ENTRANCE
CONTROL ON OTHER
SIDE

SSGT RAMON HAMMEL
AIC TERRY LOWERY

Left Making sure that all the systems are aligned before departure is a pre-requisite for all F-15 pilots, and a subject that will be taught over and over again to the budding Eagle drivers by the 325th TTW's instructors. Sitting in the hot Florida sunshine can drain most people's will to work, but occupying the greenhouse environment of an aircraft cockpit wearing all the necessary equipment can be almost unbearable. The introduction of the new lightweight moulded helmets have made a difference, although one wonders how effective they might be should the pilot be forced to eject

Above The 1st and 2nd TFTS initially received F-15A and F-15B variants of the Eagle, but following the transition of the 95th TFTS in 1988 the unit began receiving the upgraded F-15C and D-models. The jet depicted here, 75-0044, sports the yellow fin tip of the 2nd TFTS and has spent its entire career as a student training platform, first with the 58th TTW and then the 405th, before re-assignment to Tyndall. However, quite a number of early A-model Eagles have been retired to AMARC in the past year, whilst others have been sold to Israel

The 325th FWW was redesignated 325th TTW on 15 October 1983 to reflect its changing role, and the impending conversion to the F-15. At the same time the 1st and 2nd TFTSs were activated, with the first aeroplane, 74-0103, being delivered on 7 December 1983 by Brig Gen Charles A Horner. The 95th FITS, still operating the venerable T-33A, retired its jets five years later and converted to the F-15 in January 1988, becoming the 95th TFTS in the process.

The Eagle first entered the world of ADTAC when the 48th FIS at Langley AFB traded its F-106 Delta Darts in for the F-15A at the end of 1981, the first two aircraft (76-0087 and 76-0088) being delivered on 10 August 1981; the second unit to stand up was the 318th FIS at McChord AFB in September 1983. The final regular CONUS-assigned air force ADTAC unit to transition to the F-15 was the 5th FIS at Minot AFB in late 1984. This was to be followed by the 57th FIS at Keflavik as part of Air Forces Iceland in 1985.

The aircraft's period of tenure with the command was very brief, however, as all three CONUS units had stood down by the end of the decade. This allowed a number of ADTAC-gained ANG squadrons to convert onto surplus F-15As. The 101st FIS at Otis ANG received the jets originally assigned on the 5th FIS in September 1987, followed by the 123rd FIS at Portland, Oregon, who took on those previously with the 318th FIS, leaving the 48th FIS at Langley to become the final ADC squadron in the United States.

Other ANG units did transition to the F-15, although they retained their Tactical Fighter Squadron titles. The first to receive the Eagle within this group was the 122nd TFS, Louisiana ANG, located at NAS New Orleans, during June 1985. They were followed by the 128th TFS, Georgia ANG, in May 1986, the 199th TFS, Hawaii ANG, in March 1987 and finally the 110th TFS, Missouri ANG, in 1991.

The trend of identifying units as tactical or interceptor was to come to an end in October 1991, post-*Desert Storm*, when all units became fighter squadrons (FS) and TFW's FW's, bringing to an end the title of 'Interceptor' within the USAF.

However, back in October 1986 the USAF announced that the F-16 had been chosen to replace the aging F-106 and F-4 currently in use with the ANG fighter interceptor squadrons. This decision was taken after assessing the other options available, the most desirable being the use of the F-15, which was discounted when it was perceived that insufficient airframes would be available to re-equip all the squadrons. Equally, the proposed re-engined and up-graded F-4 Phantom II was dropped because of insufficient fatigue life remaining on the airframes to justify an expensive modernisation programme, whilst the final option was the F-20 Tigershark; the latter's range and armament options were considered inadequate.

Above right The 57th FIS is the last remaining former ADC asset, being the survivor of successive rounds of defence cuts – its unique location in Iceland has no doubt been the deciding factor in its retention. The unit traded its F-4E Phantom IIs in for the C-model Eagle in 1986 when the jets were transferred from the 1st TFW at Langley AFB. These were replaced within the structure of the 1st by later production C-models. 80-0050 / IS is seen here in plan view, photographed from the Tyndall control tower during the 1988 *William Tell* competition, and it is interesting to note that the aircraft has lost the normal blue eagle band on the inner surface of the fin, and sports a low-vis Black Knights badge on the port intake

Right F-15C 80-0043 was inherited from the 1st TFW at Langley, but has since been transferred to the 57th FWW at Nellis AFB following the 57th FIS's reduction in size during 1992. In this shot, which was taken at Alconbury in October 1988, the conformal tanks can be clearly seen – these devices are not commonly used by either CONUS or USAFE units

Therefore, a modified and modernised F-16 was chosen, with initial conversion being carried out by General Dynamics at Fort Worth on a prototype pattern aircraft.

The programme called for some 269 block 15 F-16A and F-16B airframes to be modified by the USAF at the Ogden Air Logistics Center, Hill AFB, Utah. All the ADF jets were to be brought up to the Operational Capabilities Upgrade (OCU) avionics standard, which was to include: 1) modifications to the Westinghouse AN/APG-66 radar to provide continuous wave illumination (enabling the aircraft to be equipped with medium-range radar-guided air-to-air missiles); 2) addition of radar software modifications to improve small target detection; 3) addition of a radar/head-up display visual identification mode; 4) installation of a 250 watt, 150,000 candle-power night identification spotlight below the threat warning antenna on the port side of the nose (not fitted to ADF F-16Bs); 5) addition of a Bendix/King AN/ARC-200 high-frequency radar warning receiver (fitted in the fin, which causes the rudder servo actuators to be located side-by-side instead of on top of the other, thus giving the F-16A ADF a distinctive horizontal bulge near the base of the fin on both sides, but not fitted to the F-16B); and 6) the installation of the Teledyne/E-Systems Mk XII Advanced IFF9, identified by the addition of a four-blade antenna atop the fuselage just forward of the cockpit, and another beneath

Left Painted in its original guise, with the blue band containing a wolf's head, this 57th FIS Eagle taxies out in company with another F-15C during the unit's deployment to RAF Alconbury as part of the NATO *Elder Forest* air defence exercises. During this period, the jets, aided by the conformal tanks and inflight refuelling, were to complete four- to five-hour CAP missions. The addition of the fuel and sensor tactical (FAST) pack conformal fuel tanks, with a capacity of 5000 lbs, is comforting to a pilot whose normal arctic operating environment is virtually devoid of diversionary airfields. The external fuel cells allow the 57th FIS to effectively police the Iceland gap, the unit undertaking patrol handovers from Norwegian controlled air space to the east and Canadian controlled airspace from Goose Bay, Labrador, to the West

Above The latest squadron to adopt the F-15 Eagle is the 390th FS as part of the 366th Wing at Mountain Home AFB. The unit is the first of a new USAF tactical package which sees all the necessary types within a frontline wing under one umbrella so that they can train together and, if the need arises, deploy together. The aircraft for this squadron are the last F-15Cs delivered to the USAF from the 1986 fiscal budget. They were originally allocated to the 33rd TFW, and in particular the 59th TFS, until re-assignment during 1992. As there have been no further deliveries of air supremacy F-15s to the air force to make up for those transferred jets, it may well be that one of the Eglin squadrons will de-activate the intake.

The first USAF modified aircraft came in the shape of F-16B 81-0817 in October 1988, which had spent the early part of its career with the 6512th Test Squadron at Edwards AFB — it was returned to the unit for evaluation following the upgrade. The first single-seat jet, F-16A 81-0693, formerly of the 57th FWW, was delivered to the ANG/AFRES Test Centre (under the auspices of the Arizona ANG) at Tucson ANGB at around the same time. The 3246th Test Wing at Eglin AFB received F-16A ADF 81-0761, one of its former mounts, for armament trials in late 1988, whilst the 422nd TES at Nellis AFB made use of F-16A ADFs 81-0772 and 82-0956 to conduct Tactics Development and Evaluations (TD&E).

The first F-16 ADF to be assigned to the Air National Guard came in the shape of 81-0801, an A-model which was delivered to the 114th TFTS/Oregon ANG at Kingsley Field on 1 February 1989. This unit had responsibility for training all F-16 ADF pilots for ANG squadrons. The first operational unit to receive the modified aircraft was the 194th FIS, California ANG, at Fresno, which took F-16B 82-1048 on charge on 13 April 1989. The 11 air defence units involved have sent two aircraft at a time to the Ogden centre, and by 25 October 1991 some 222 airframes had been modified to ADF configuration.

The F-16 had in fact begun service entry with the former ADTAC squadrons before the ADF programme actually got under way. The 159th FIS, Florida ANG, received its first jets during August 1986 when F-16As 80-0562 and 80-0565 were loaned for maintenance familiarisation. This unit was preceded by the 134th TFS, Vermont ANG, which transitioned to the F-16A following the inactivation of the 16th TFS/388th TFW, and although nominally a tactical unit at this stage, it was to revert back to its ADTAC commitment shortly afterwards.

Today, the whole question of maintaining a committed force of air defence units in the United States is under question, and it may be that with the growing pressure to reduce defence spending such a luxury will

Right The first ADC unit to receive the F-15 Eagle in early 1982 was the 48th FIS at Langley AFB. The jets themselves were drawn from the 1st TFW which was at that time upgrading to the newer C-model. Although the 48th was to be absorbed into the new 1st AF structure and begin receiving LY tailcodes, this did not guarantee their future. In the six years that they operated the Eagle the unit transferred out of 20th AD control to that of the 23rd AD on 1 March 1983, and then to the 24th AD when the 23rd deactivated in 1987. 76-0113 is seen lifting off from Tyndall's far runway in 1982, the Eagle having already seen service with both the 49th TFW and the 1st TFW prior to its ADC posting. It was later handed over to the 199th FS, Hawaii ANG, as a replacement for older 1974 fiscal machines

be dispensed with. It is significant to note, however, that once again the first F-16 kill for the USAF came from what had been a tactical squadron when, during Operation *Southern Watch*, Lt Col Gary North, commander of the 33rd FS/363rd FW deployed to Dhahran, shot down an Iraqi MiG-25 on 27 December 1992 in F-16D 90-0778/SW. The intercept resulted in the first kill not only by a USAF F-16 but also with the AIM-120A AMRAAM missile; the MiG-25 was one of a pair that strayed well south of the 32nd parallel. A 23rd FS/52nd FW F-16C, 86-0262/SP, shot down an Iraqi MiG-29 in the north of the country on 17 January 1993.

The reduction in committed air defence units within the ANG has already begun with announcements that the 128th FS, Georgia ANG, will transition to the B-1B Lancer and re-locate to Robins AFB, and the 136th FS, New York ANG, will convert to the KC-135R. The day of the pure manned-interceptor is, perhaps, nearly over.

Above F-15B 75-0086 seen taxying out at Tyndall in October 1982. The unit was a regular visitor to the base as the 48th held alert duty here, and following its demise this particular jet was to find itself assigned to Tyndall on a more permanent basis as part of the 325th TTW. Today, it serves with the 128th FS, Georgia ANG

Above Although the 128th TFS first received the F-15A in May 1986 when aircraft 74-0128 was delivered from the 405th TTW at Luke AFB, it retained its former title rather than adopting an air defence FIS mantle. This reflected the changing role of the air superiority fighter in working with strike assets in the protective sweep or CAP roles. This did not deter the unit from making the most of its prestigious mount, however, and they participated in the 1988 *William Tell* alongside formidable frontline opposition provided by the 18th, 33rd and 49th TFWs, as well as the 57th FIS from Iceland

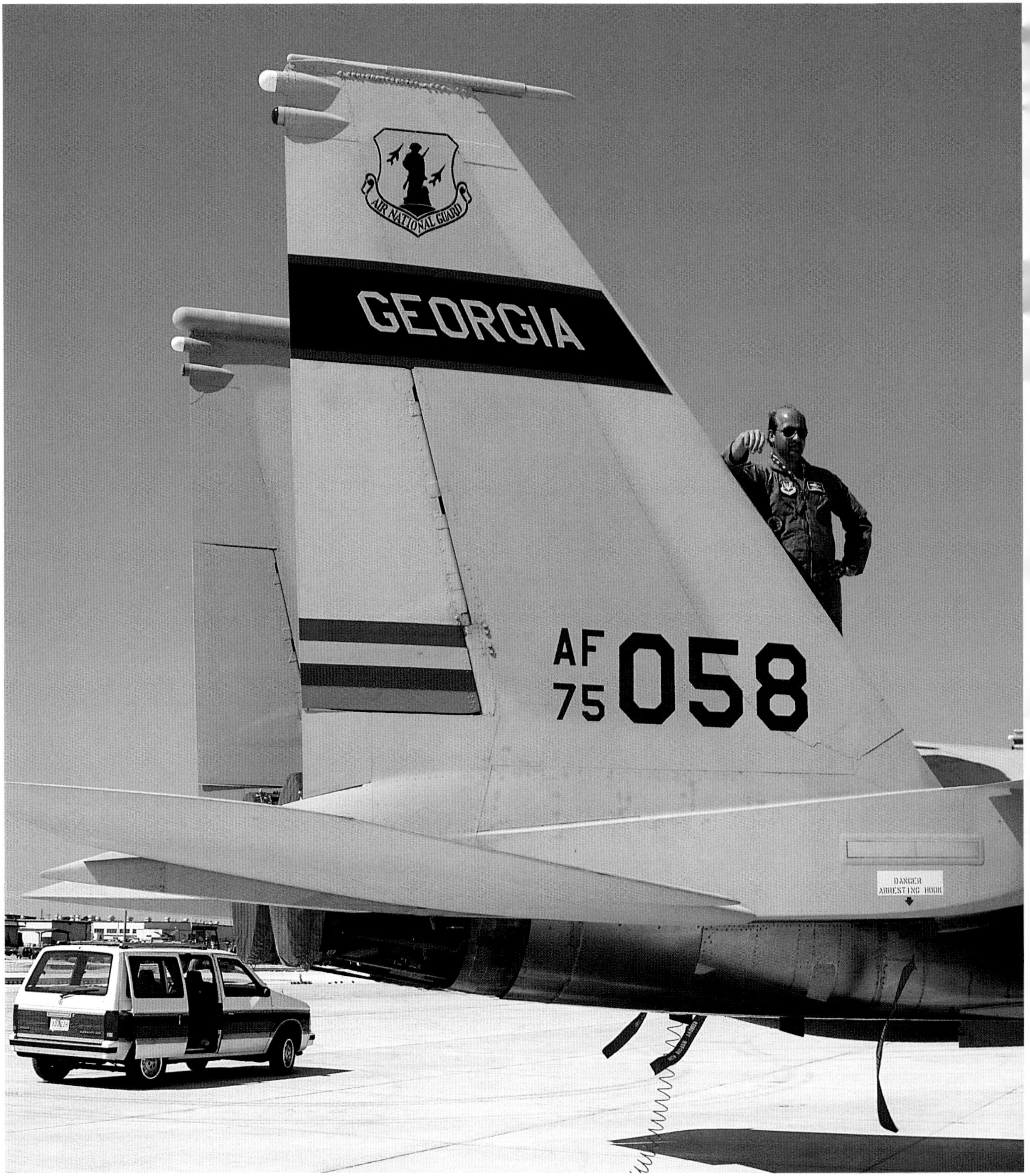

AIR NATIONAL GUARD
GEORGIA
AF
75
058
DANGER
ARRESTING HOOK

Left Capt Steve 'Hose'm' Beck poses by the tail of his Georgia F-15A during the 1988 *William Tell*. The jet concerned, 75-0058, is a former USAFE machine having been delivered to the 22nd TFS/36th TFW at Bitburg on 8 June 1977. It was acquired by the 128th TFS by way of the 1st TFW at Langley AFB, and in this shot the aircraft is painted in the relatively high visibility colours of the period. Today, the unit's jets wear a series of dull pastel grey shades, with all stencilling in outline only. Since the formation of Air Combat Command (ACC) the unit has also begun utilising the recently assigned 'GA' tailcode

Above A pair of AIM-9L Sidewinder missiles on the starboard wing pylons of a 128th TFS F-15A Eagle. The missile weighs roughly 160 lbs, with a 10-lb warhead. It is nine feet long and can track a target for around 12 miles, although the effective killing range is more likely to be two. The 128th is to lose its F-15s in the not too distant future and convert to the B-1B Lancer. This change in task will also see the unit re-locate for the very first time in its history, the 128th probably moving to Robins AFB

Above Final attempts at making the *William Tell* competition something of an occasion. Although most jets involved in the 1988 meet were in pristine condition, they lacked the little touches that were formerly part of the event. The Georgia boys did at least all sport distinctive patches on their flight suits, although with velcro attachment, they could be removed at a moment's notice

Right To the pilot of any fighter aircraft, probably the one item that holds prime importance is the ejection seat as if push comes to shove this may be the only thing between life and death. Here, a McDonnell Douglas ACES II 'zero-zero' seat is raised along its rails to facilitate maintenance. The 'remove before flight' tags ensure that although the seat is armed it remains safe

D/C/C SSGT K. A. ASNICAR

A/D/C/C SGT C. L. CAVALLI

RESCUE

Above In spite of a general toning down of colour schemes, the 178th FS at Fargo, North Dakota, have managed to retain some colour by the inclusion of the 'Happy Hooligans' logo in a red band on the fin. The unit began the transition onto the F-16 in 1989, and it is thought it received ADF modified jets from the outset. 81-0781, depicted here, was a former 388th TFW machine which was returned to the Ogden ALC when that unit began transition to the F-16C model. It was from Ogden that it was taken on charge by the 178th FS sometime in early to mid 1990

Above Akin to the 178th FS, the 171st FS transitioned from the F-4D to the F-16A in late 1989. However, unlike the 178th, it is believed that it first received unmodified jets which were then despatched to the Ogden ALC for conversion. In fact, as late as January 1991 unmodified aeroplanes were still on strength with the unit, F-16A 81-0717 being lost in a crash at this time. As jets were returned from Ogden they began receiving the standard 171st FS chequered markings, although to date this decoration has failed to live up to the unit's more colourful F-4 days. In this shot the distinctive bulge beneath the tail, which houses the Bendix/King AN/ARC-200 high frequency RWR, easily identifies the aircraft as ADF modified

Above The Florida ANG were originally slated to receive the F-4D, but following the decision by ADTAC to de-activate the 87th FIS at K I Sawyer AFB, their allocated aircraft were diverted to Duluth to enable the latter unit's alert commitment to be maintained. The 159th FIS, in the meantime, soldiered on with the Delta Dart until conversion to the F-16A in August 1986. The ADF variant was not received until mid 1989 when the unit began ferrying aircraft back to Hill AFB for modification. However, as a sign of the times, the 159th FS has recently had its two alert commitments – Jacksonville and Homestead – inactivated, casting some doubt on the unit's future

Left This ADF F-16B is operated by the 114th FS at Kingsley Field, which serves as the ANG ADF training unit. The 114th has an above average mix of F-16A and F-16B aeroplanes to accommodate the training task, and 82-1027, depicted here with the attractive Oregon Eagle marking, was received from the 195th TFTS, Arizona ANG, who in turn had collected it from the 57th FWW at Nellis AFB where this particular shot was taken. The Oregon unit began transitioning onto the F-16 in 1988 from the aging, but much loved, F-4C. It received the ADF version in early 1989

Left The personal mount of Col Gary Kaiser, CO of the 178th FS/119th FG at Fargo, North Dakota, F-16A-ADF 82-0926 was another former 421st TFS/388th TFW aeroplane inherited by the unit in early 1990, following modification in the co-located Ogden ALC. In October 1989 there were some 19 F-16s under conversion in the Air Logistics Center, including 81-0699 destined for the 'Happy Hooligans', this aeroplane having been transferred from the 31st TFW at Homestead AFB, Florida

Drones, Hacks and Gate Guards

The use of aerial targets has long been a vital training aid for the fighter pilot, be it the traditional towed sleeve for air-to-air gunnery, or the more modern radar reflective dart. The advent of radar and missile technology has meant that targets have had to keep pace with these advances.

Tracking by radar is good practice for air defenders, and is the prime source of training. The introduction of missile simulation pods has given pilots the ability to learn about weapon parameters, whilst the development of the Air Combat Manoeuvring Instrumented Range (ACMI) has proven tactics. However, there is no real substitute for actually firing a missile or shooting a gun at an adversary. Fortunately, such scenarios occur very infrequently which does of course make training for such eventualities rather difficult.

Equally, the price of a modern day missile makes the firing of rounds for training almost prohibitive, but such is the requirement for air defenders to be in a position to achieve a kill each time they are be called upon, the costs have to be accepted. Day to day passive training hones the necessary skills, but occasionally the fighter pilot has to try it out for real, or at least as near to real as training can allow.

The advent of the drone allowed this aim to be achieved. In 1958 the USAF introduced the radio controlled Q-2A unmanned target and an electronic scoring system called PARAMI, which marked the changes occurring in the air defence world. Later came the BQM-34A/F Firebee turbojet-powered drones, first introduced in 1959, and then ultimately the introduction of real aircraft targets.

The use of redundant fighter airframes in the USAF drone programme came about following studies of the successful conversion of former USAF F-86F and T-33A aircraft for the US Navy. At the same time, support for an

Left A line-up of Delta Dart tails at Tyndall AFB in 1992. In spite of the red fins, a colour applied to denote conversion to QF-106 standard, the rudders are a dead giveaway as to their once proud owners. The first jet, however, still retains complete 5th FIS markings, a unit that said goodbye to the Dart in 1984 and inactivated completely in 1988. F-106B 57-2545 is retained by the 84th TS in its former markings as a pilot currency trainer, and has not been converted by TRACOR Flight Systems

expendable supersonic drone was forthcoming from the US Army who needed targets for the trials of new air defence missile systems, in particular Patriot, which were being conducted on the White Sands Missile Range in New Mexico. The army had, up to this point, been utilising subsonic ex-RCAF Canadair-built Sabre 5/6s, converted to drone standard by Flight Systems at Mojave.

The contract to convert the surplus F-102 Delta Daggers to drone configuration was awarded to Sperry Flight Systems in March 1973. The initial funding covered the conversion of two F-102As, 56-1443 and 56-1081, to QF-102A specs for crew training and system evaluation under a programme called *Pave Deuce*. This was followed by three further airframes – 56-1475, 56-1347 and 56-1400 – which were modified to the same standard, plus TF-102A 56-2317 for type currency.

The first conversions were carried out at Sperry's Crestview facility in Florida, but the programme was later moved to Litchfield Park (the former US Navy storage airfield) in Arizona. This move placed the Sperry facility in close proximity to its main source of supply, the storage centre at Davis-Monthan AFB, to where most F-102s had been retired.

In 1973, when the project was first started, there were still six users of the venerable 'Deuce' — the 102nd FIS, 146th FIS, 176th FIS, 190th FIS, 199th FIS and 157th FIS — which allowed a few aeroplanes to be delivered without passing through the storage programme at MASDC. However, the bulk of the jets involved were to be drawn from storage and returned to a limited flying category before the Sperry technicians became involved.

Next came the conversion of some 65 airframes to PQM-102A standard for use by the 475th TS of the Aerospace Defense Weapons Center at Tyndall AFB, and the joint US Army/USAF 6580th TW at Holloman AFB. The latter were to be primarily involved in surface-to-air missile testing over the White Sands Missile Range facility.

The conversion of the 'Deuce' continued well into 1982, with some 124 airframes forming the third part of the contract and being designated PQM-102B. The difference between the three variants meant that the QF-102A was a man-rated drone only, the PQM-102A had remote control equipment fitted in the cockpit, whilst in the PQM-102B the same kit was updated and repositioned in the nose. The types were identifiable by the Sperry three-digit conversion numbers, the first five being 501-2 and 601-3; the PQM-102A 604-667/700 and PQM-102B 701-824 accounted for a further 194 airframes altogether.

Use of the *Pave Deuce* with the Air Force continued until 14 July 1983 when the last PQM-102B sortie was made by the 475th TS at Tyndall AFB. The aircraft involved, 56-1175 '793', was tasked as a target for a quartet of 4th TFW F-4E Phantom IIs being controlled by the 4756th Air Defense Squadron. However, in spite of the efforts of both controller and aircrews,

Above right QF-106A 57-2506 was formerly in use with the 101st FIS at Otis ANGB, and sports an appropriate unit code number by the jet pipe. This aircraft was stored at Davis-Monthan with the park code 'FN169', before being passed to TRACOR as the 107th example to be converted to drone configuration. Alongside it, 59-0054 is totally devoid of markings from its previous owner, although it was last noted in use at McChord AFB with the 318th FIS. It preceded its ramp mate onto the Mojave conversion line by six airframes

Right Tyndall's 100-ft high control tower is blessed with an elevator. Ten years ago a shot on a ramp with a tall red/white chequered structure within the frame would have instantly placed the photographer at Tyndall AFB. Today, it has been repainted in this sandy colour and overlooks not only the operational apron, but what was once the main parking area for the T-33As, now home to the 84th Test Squadron's QF-106s. The 'Darts' in the foreground were clearly once used by the 87th, 186th and 101st FISs, but they also sport AMARC park codes. Life expectancy is but a mere ten missions!

the 'Dagger' refused such an ignominious end and the aircraft was recovered, albeit with a damaged wing, to Tyndall. The jet was then transferred with another survivor to Holloman AFB, where it was thought the army would achieve the desired results.

As a follow on to *Pave Deuce* Sperry was awarded a contract to begin conversion of the F-100D to a drone configuration. Ten aircraft, 56-3414/092, 55-3610/093, 56-3048/094, 55-3669/095, 56-2979/096, 56-3984/097, 56-2912/098, 56-2978/099, 56-3324/100 and 56-3861 were delivered to the Litchfield plant between September 1980 and March 1981 as research and development test beds. The first two were designated YQF-100Ds, the others QF-100Ds, except 097, which was a QF-100F (ex-F-100F 56-3861) retained as a training platform.

Sperry was to convert 80 'Huns' to drone configuration before the contract was retendered and awarded to TRACOR Flight Systems Inc at Mojave. They took over production of the remaining F-100 drones from 1 January 1985 and were to convert a further 129 aircraft. However, prior to this occurring various command changes had happened affecting the drone squadron at Tyndall.

Above Former 176th FIS F-102A Delta Dagger 56-1223 from Traux Field, Madison, Wisconsin, lifts off wearing the new guise of a PQM-102B with the 475th WEG. Often flown with a pilot, many of the sorties carried out by the unit see their jets providing targets for simulated intercepts. Equally, pure drone sorties are not flown from the main active airfield at Tyndall in case things do not go according to plan. Adjacent to the main facility is the drone field, and such flights take place from there on a heading that will not conflict with the active airfield

Above A number of camouflaged former 157th FIS F-102As are seen on the receipt and despatch apron at MASDC during late 1978 including 56-1086, 56-1193 and 56-1083, which are being prepared for ferrying to Litchfield Park for conversion to *Pave Deuce* PQM-102B specs. The three jets seen here became conversion '721', '718' and '727' respectively, whilst the nearest example quite clearly displays its park code of 4FJ354. 194 of these aircraft were converted for use at both Tyndall and Holloman AFBs, with the final sortie from Tyndall taking place on 14 July 1983

As mentioned previously, TAC had taken over from ADCOM in 1979, with the ADWC being redesignated 325th FWW on 1 July 1981 and 2nd FITS to 2nd FWS on 1 February 1982. Then on 15 October 1983 both the 475th TSS and 4756th ADS were inactivated to be replaced by the 475th Weapons Evaluation Group (WEG), which had under its command the 81st Range Control Squadron, 82nd TATS (which was transferred from the 325th FWW) and the 83rd FWS. The 325th FWW became the 325th TTW on the same date. The 475th WEG effectively took control of all drone activity both manned and unmanned targets, which involved the supersonic QF-100Ds and BQM-34Fs, the subsonic BQM-34As and TDU-25B towed targets.

The final command change to affect Tyndall AFB occurred in 1986 when ADTAC became the 1st Air Force, although there was still the restructuring of the USAF to come. However, by January 1986 some 46 QF-100Ds had been destroyed. The average life of a drone was considered to be ten missions, during which time it would act as target. From that point onwards it was considered expendable and the return of the investment equalled.

In December 1985, following the retirement of more than 100 F-106 Delta Darts to AMARC, it was announced that under an air force programme called *Pacer Six*, around 200 of these airframes would be converted into drones for use by the air force between 1988 and 1995. The first of these, F-106B 59-0152 and F-106A 56-0454, had been sent to TRACOR Flight Systems at Mojave from AMARC on 28 October 1986, the former taking the conversion code 'AD101'.

On 13 March 1992 two former 3rd TFW F-4G Phantom II aircraft, 69-7261 and 69-7301, arrived at Mojave from AMARC destined to become part of the follow-on programme from *Pacer Six*. These two aeroplanes were re-designated QF-4Gs in April, when it was made known that all-told some eight airframes had been despatched to the company for trials. It was also reported that of the approximate 1000 Phantom IIs remaining in the USAF inventory, 900 of which were already in store, the RF-4Cs, F-4Es and F-4Gs would be converted initially, and that it was unlikely that the F-4Ds would receive the same treatment.

Back at air force HQ, with the structural changes instituted post-*Desert Storm*, the Air Combat Command (ACC), which had taken over most of the former TAC assets, took this opportunity to reorganise its test and evaluation units. Amongst the changes was the activation of the 79th Test and Evaluation Group at Eglin AFB, which not only controlled its own 85th TES (formerly 4485th TS), but also the 84th TS, which held responsibility for the QF-106, BQM-34 and MQM-107 drones at Tyndall AFB.

Also associated with intercept training at Tyndall AFB (as well as most other ADC units) were the venerable T-33A Shooting Stars. The aircraft doubled as both squadron hacks and low cost dissimilar targets, the 95th FITS at Tyndall holding a dual role of training T-33 pilots as well as assisting in the training of tactics to all ADC users. The jet was also used by the 82nd TATS at Tyndall as a drone control and chase mount. As a precaution, when a drone is flown by remote control it is followed by a chase plane during the take-off and landing phase.

The 'T-bird', very much a legacy of a bygone era, outlived all the Century Series fighters, and to some degree became a source of embarrassment to the modern day USAF. The role of training faded early after TAC absorbed ADC, with the 84th FIS at Castle AFB being redesignated 84th FITS on 1 July 1981 to encompass all T-33A training activities, a role it took over from the Tyndall-based squadron. The 460th FITS was reassigned to Tyndall AFB on 15 January 1982, before being inactivated on 15 October 1982. However, the T-33A was to soldier on both at Tyndall and at other former ADCOM units until around 1987, when the 48th FIS at Langley AFB, which was by this time operating the F-15A Eagle, retired its last five aeroplanes, transferring four of them to the Mexican Air Force.

Right Most missiles have a proximity fuse, and to preserve the lifespan of these aircraft TRACOR Flight Systems have devised a wing-mounted hot pod system which gives the drone a better chance of survival. The AIM-9L Sidewinder missile will close on the main heat source, which is generally the engine exhaust, but by creating a heat source of greater magnitude on the wing tip the seeker head will direct the missile to this point, and the proximity fuse will detonate the warhead close to the wing rather than the jet pipe. This gives the drone a chance of surviving the attack, the target having been manoeuvring like any manned fighter to avoid being shot down. Ten sorties are considered a drone lifespan, after which they are fair game

Above At any one time there are around 40 to 50 drones available to the 84th TS. During October 1988 when this shot was taken, there were some 40 QF-100Ds, two QF-106As, a single QF-106B and three proficiency trainers in evidence. By the beginning of that year 46 QF-100Ds had been destroyed, but production had converted at least 236 examples. However, by March 1992 the totals had reversed, with 43 QF-106s being present as opposed to only seven QF-100s, indicating the turnover in target use. The examples pictured here include QF-100D 56-3112 '342', QF-106A 59-0119 'AD106', with a road runner character on the nose wheel door, and QF-106B 59-0152 'AD101'

Above right F-100F 63-3861 taxies back to the drone park at Tyndall following a proficiency flight by one of the 47th WEG test pilots. The jet, once the proud possession of the 182nd TFS at Kelly AFB, arrived at Tyndall at the start of the QF-100 programme. On the rear fuselage can be seen the former AMARC park code, whilst in the background ADWC can be seen to be supporting both F-106s with 2nd FITS and T-33As with 95th FITS, although the TAC badges indicate that it was late in their careers

Right 'Lindberghs Own', an inscription lost on the 'Hun' in its present predicament, having survived from its former life with the 131st TFW Missouri ANG in the 1970s. However, in spite of its intended significance, it clearly snipes at the missile and gun threat in pertaining to be a trusty, defiant steed. The jet concerned was QF-100D 56-3412

Above A Firebee, or BQM-34, seen here alongside a pair of 82nd TATS launches used to recover these turbojet drones from a watery grave in the Gulf of Mexico

Left Electronic Counter Measures (ECM) play an important part in a high threat scenario, and to add a touch of realism to air defence training, such services have been offered in a number of forms. One example was the EB-57B/E used by the 117th, 134th and 4677th DSESs at Forbes ANGB, Burlington IAP and Malmstrom AFB respectively, which could carry out communications jamming and chaff/flare deception. However, akin to the Century Series fighters, the 'Canberra' was also somewhat long-in-the-tooth, and by 1978 only the guard unit in Vermont remained operational on the type, and they were to retire the jet in October 1981. EB-57B 52-1521 from the 'Green Mountain Boys' is depicted arriving back at Tyndall following a *William Tell* Profile IV sortie

At Tyndall itself, the 95th FITS was redesignated 95th TFTS and became the third F-15 squadron within the 325th TTW. The task of providing target facilities for the resident and deployed squadrons was passed to civilian contract in October 1988 when Flight International took over the job using a number of Mitsubishi Mu-2 turboprop aircraft.

The Air National Guard also used the venerable 'T-bird' as a support aircraft, as well as veteran piston-engined twins like the C-131 and C-7, which doubled as transport for the State Governor. Generally speaking, these support aircraft also adopted the same bright scheme as the frontline assets. This practice still continues today, the new C-12s and C-26s received by the units proudly wearing distinctive state colours..

With no less than 40 squadrons having operated the Delta Dagger, 20 the Delta Dart and 20 the Voodoo, it is not surprising that a great number of these types can be found in the most unlikely of locations as memorials to a distant past. Sometimes, thoughts of preservation came along after the hardware was available to be preserved, so many units have had to reclaim wrecks from range areas, or adapted later marks of aircraft to represent their own period. Fortunately, we are now much more preservation minded, and losses that have occurred in the past hopefully will not occur in the future.

Right The Martin derivative of the Canberra, with its tandem seating arrangement, served long and hard in a variety of roles due to its legendary adaptability. It is through such electrifying names as 'Patricia Lynn', 'Doom Pussy', 'Tropic Moon' and 'Diamond Lil' that the type is best remembered, but for the interceptors of ADCOM, it was their annoying habit of upsetting the best radar attack solutions the fighter could offer that will remain uppermost in their minds. The 134th DSES Vermont ANG were the final users of this multi-purpose aeroplane, a type that still holds affection for many that flew it

Above First the 97th and then the 95th FITS operated the T-33A as part of the ADWC. Here, aircraft 58-0565 waits in turn amongst the other 32 examples present on this day in 1978, whilst in the background can be seen *William Tell* competitors from the 3rd TFW, 178th FIS and 111st FIS. The 'T-bird' was used as drone chaser in the take-off and landing phases of pilotless flight

Left All in pristine condition, a trio of T-33s line up on the transient ramp at Tyndall AFB whilst F-15A Eagles from the 49th TFW await the call in the background. The nearest example, 58-0673, in an unusual white scheme, comes from the 48th FIS and was one of the last five T-33s active in the regular Air Force, being retired during March 1987. Parked next to it is an example from the resident 95th FITS, whilst at the end of the line comes a CT-133 from VU-32, prior to its fitment with a threat emitter. On the horizon can be seen a number of *Pave Deuce* PQM-102s

Above The deadly game of air combat relies on seeing before being seen. In today's world of electronic gadgetry many engagements occur without the adversaries ever visually spotting each other. However, in the close air environment watching one's 'six' is all important. Maj 'K P' McNeil looks back over his right shoulder prior to committing the jet to a manoeuvre

Above right Maintained in a condition that any unit would be proud of, the 'Happy Hooligans' support Convair C-131D glistens in the afternoon sun at Tyndall AFB. Most units participating at *William Tell* received goodwill visits from family and friends, a service offered by the unit in the State Governor's transport when undertaking normal resupply flights

Right Not many F-15s have so far been preserved as the jet is, after all, still in production, with even the early variants still in use. However, a few well-worn examples have been retired including 71-0281, which is preserved at Langley AFB, and 74-0124, which is in the aircraft and armaments museum at Eglin AFB. This example, 74-0095, is preserved at Tyndall AFB in a somewhat anonymous state, despite its service with the 58th, 405th and 325th TTWs during its career

Above As a returning Eagle banks hard over the top of a preserved F-104 Starfighter, this photograph serves as a reminder that this Century Series interceptor was not featured in this volume. The jet found little favour with ADC due to a series of fatal crashes, plus its lack of endurance. In fact the Starfighter only served with four ADC units, the 83rd, 319th, 331st and 538th FISs, although the jets were passed onto the following ANG units; the 151st, 157th, 197th and 337th FISs. This did not stop preservation-minded people from gathering up the last of these jets to operate in the USA and adopt them as part of their heritage. Unfortunately, very few F-104As survived to be preserved, so units had to make do with the F-104C version that had been exclusively utilised by the tactical units. This particular jet, 56-0919, is preserved at Tyndall alongside a number of other types that operated from the base

Unit Listings, Specifications and Line Drawings

Convair F-102

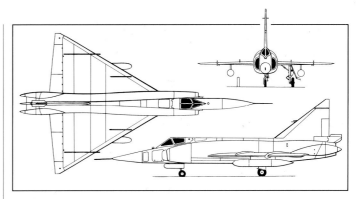

Origin: Convair Division of General Dynamics, San Diego, California

Type: (F) single-seat all-weather interceptor, (TF) trainer, (QF) manned RPV (remotely piloted vehicle), (PQM) drone target

Engine: One 17,200 lb (7802 kg) thrust Pratt & Whitney J57-23 two-shaft afterburning turbojet

Dimensions: Span 28 ft 1 ½ in (11.6 m); length (F-102A) 68 ft 5 in (20.83 m), (TF-102A) 63 ft 4 ½ in (19.3 m); height (F-102A) 21 ft 2 ½ in (6.45 m), (TF-102A) 20 ft 7 in (6.27 m); wing area 661.5 sq ft (61.46 m²)

Weights: Empty (F-102A) 19,050 lb (8630 kg); loaded (F-102A, clean) 27,700 lb (12,564 kg), (maximum) 31,500 lb (14,288 kg)

Performance: Maximum speed (F-102A) 825 mph (1328 km/h, Mach 1.25), (TF-102A) 646 mph (1040 km/h); initial climb (F-102A) 13,000 ft (3962 m)/min; service ceiling 54,000 ft (16,460 m); range 1350 miles (2172 km)

Armament: Air-to-air guided missiles carried in internal bay, typical full load comprising three Hughes AIM-4E Falcon beam-riders with semi-active homing and three AIM-4F with infrared homing. No armament in TF, QF, or PQM

History: First flight (YF-102) 24 October 1953, (YF-102A) 20 December 1954, (TF) 8 November 1955, (QF) mid-1974, (PQM) 1975

Convair F-102A Delta Dagger Units

2nd FIS	52nd FIG	Suffolk County AFB, New York	1957–1959
4th FIS	39th AD	Misawa AB, Japan	1960–1965
5th FIS		Minot AFB, North Dakota	1957–1960
16th FIS	51st FIW	Naha AB, Okinawa	1959–1964
18th FIS		Wurtsmith AFB, Michigan	1957–1960
25th FIS	51st FIW	Naha AB, Okinawa	1959–1960
27th FIS	4711th ADW	Griffiths AFB, New York	1957–1959
31st FIS	9th AD	Elmendorf AFB, Alaska	1956
32nd FIS	86th FIW	Soesterberg AB, Holland [1]	1960–1969
37th FIS	14th FIG	Ethan Allen AFB, Burlington, Vermont	1957–1960
40th FIS	41st AD	Yokota AB, Japan	1960–1965
47th FIS	15th FIG	Niagara Falls Airport, New York	1958–1960
48th FIS	4710th ADW	Langley AFB, Virginia	1957–1960
57th FIS		NAS Keflavik, Iceland	1962–1973
59th FIS	64th AD	Goose Bay CFB, Labrador	1960–1967
61st FIS		Traux Field, Wisconsin	1957–1960
64th FIS	25th AD	Paine Field, Washington [2]	1957–1969
68th FIS	41st AD	Itazuke AB, Japan	1959–1964
71st FIS	1st FIG	Selfridge AFB, Michigan	1958–1960
76th FIS	23rd FIG	Westover AFB, Massachusetts	1961–1963
82nd FIS	28th AD	Travis AFB, California [3]	1957–1971
86th FIS	79th FIG	Youngstown Airport, Ohio	1957–1960
87th FIS		Lockbourne AFB, Ohio	1958–1960
95th FIS	4710th ADW	Andrews AFB, Maryland	1958–1959
102nd FIS	106th FIG	New York ANG	1972–1975
111th FIS	147th FIG	Texas ANG	1960–1975
116th FIS	141st FIG	Washington ANG	1966–1969
118th FIS	103rd FIG	Connecticut ANG	1965–1971
122nd FIS	159th FIG	Louisiana ANG	1960–1970
123rd FIS	142nd FIG	Oregon ANG	1966–1971
132nd FIS	101st FIG	Maine ANG	1969–1969
134th FIS	158th FIG	Vermont ANG	1965–1974
146th FIS	112th FIG	Pennsylvania ANG	1960–1975
151st FIS	134th FIG	Tennessee ANG	1963–1964
152nd FIS	162nd FIG	Arizona ANG	1966–1969
157th FIS	169th FIG	South Carolina ANG	1963–1975
159th FIS	125th FIG	Florida ANG	1959–1974
175th FIS	114th FIG	South Dakota ANG	1960–1970
176th FIS	115th FIG	Wisconsin ANG	1966–1974
178th FIS	119th FIG	North Dakota ANG	1966–1969
179th FIS	148th FIG	Minnesota ANG	1966–1972
182nd FIS	149th FIG	Texas ANG	1960–1969
186th FIS	120th FIG	Montana ANG	1966–1972
190th FIS	124th FIG	Idaho ANG	1964–1975
194th FIS	144th FIG	California ANG	1964–1974
196th FIS	163rd FIG	California ANG	1965–1975
199th FIS	154th FIG	Hawaii ANG	1964–1975
317th FIS	325th FIG	Elmendorf AFB Alaska	1956–1970
318th FIS	325th FIG	McChord AFB, Washington	1957–1959
323rd FIS	327th FIG	Ernest Harman AFB, Newfoundland	1957–1961
325th FIS	327th FIG	Traux Field, Wisconsin	1957–1966
326th FIS	328th FIG	Richards–Gebar AFB, Montana	1957–1967
327th FIS		George AFB, California	1956–1960
329th FIS		Sheppard AFB, Texas	1958–1960
331st FIS	329th FIG	Webb AFB, Texas	1960–1963
332nd FIS	4709th ADW	McGuire AFB, New Jersey	1957–1965
431st FIS	65th AD	Zaragosa, Spain	1960–1964
438th FIS	507th FIG	Kinross AFB, Michigan	1957–1960
456th FIS	27th AD?	Traux Field, Wisconsin	1958–1959
460th FIS	337th FIG	Portland Airport, Oregon	1958–1966
482nd FIS	83rd FDW	Seymour Johnson AFB, Virginia	1956–1965
496th FIS	86th FIW	Hahn AB, West Germany	1960–1969
497th FIS	65th AD	Torrejon AB, Spain	1960–1964
498th FIS	83rdFDW	Greiger Field, Spokane, Washington	1957–1959
509th FIS	405th FW	Clark AB, Philippines [3]	1960–1969
525th FIS	86th FIW	Bitburg AB	1959–1969
526th FIS	86th FIW	Ramstein AB, West Germany	1960–1970
3558th FIS	ATC	Perrin AFB, Texas	
4780th	ADW	Perrin AFB, Texas	

The assigned wing or division changed not only when squadrons re–located but on a number of occasions through command restructuring. The above table does not correspond with any particular point within the squadron history.

1. 32nd FIS assigned to Wheelus AFB 12/8/60 to 17/12/60.
2. Reassigned to Clark AB on 2/6/66.
3. Both the 82nd and 509th served in South East Asia from various locations including Tan Son Nhut and Da Nang. The 82nd FIS deployed from Travis AFB, California to Naha as part of the 51st FIW prior to assignment in SEA, returning to that location when the F-102 was withdrawn from theatre.

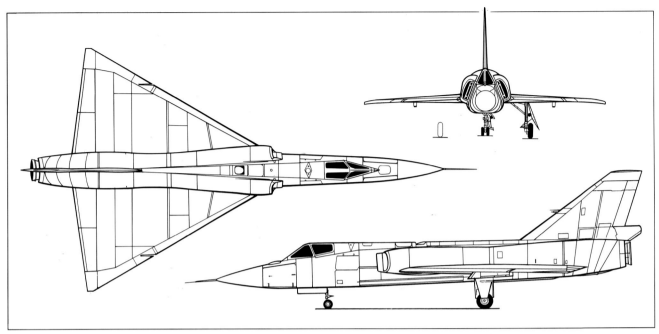

Convair F-106 Delta Dart

Origin: General Dynamics Convair Division, San Diego, California
Type: All-weather interceptor, (B) operational trainer
Engine: One 24,500 lb (11,113 kg) thrust Pratt & Whitney J75-17 afterburning turbojet
Dimensions: Span 38 ft 3 in (11.67 m); length (both) 70 ft 8 ¾ in (21.55 m); height 20 ft 3 ¼ in (6.18 m); wing area 661.5 sq ft (61.52m²)
Weights: Empty (A) about 24,420 lb (11,077 kg); loaded (normal) 34,510 lb (15,668 kg)
Peformance: Maximum speed (both) 1525 mph (2455 km/h) or Mach 2.3 at 36,000 ft (10,973 m); initial climb about 29,000 ft (8839 m)/min; service ceiling 57,000 ft (17,374 m); range with drop tanks 1800 miles (2897 km)
Armament: One 20 mm M61A1 gun, two AIM-4F plus two AIM-4G Falcons, plus one AIR-2A or -2G Genie nuclear rocket
History: First flight (aerodynamic prototype) 26 December 1956, (B) 9 April 1958; squadron delivery June 1959

Convair F–106 Delta Dart Operators

2nd FIS		Wurtsmith AFB, Michigan	1971–1973
2nd FITS	ADWC	Tyndall AFB, Florida	1974–1981
2nd FITS	325th FWW	Tyndall AFB, Florida	1981–1982
2nd FWS	325th FWW	Tyndall AFB, Florida	1982–1983
5th FIS	24th AD	Minot AFB, North Dakota	1960–1985
11th FIS	30th AD	Duluth AP , Minnesota	1960–1968
27th FIS		Loring AFB, Maine	1959–1971
48th FIS	20th AD	Langley AFB, Virginia	1960–1982
49th FIS	21st AD	Griffiths AFB, New York	1968–1987
71st FIS	26th AD	Selfridge AFB, Michigan	1960–1971
83rd FIS		Loring AFB, Maine	1971–1972
84th FIS		Hamilton AFB then Castle AFB, Cal	1968–1981
87th FIS	21st AD	K I Sawyer AFB, Michigan	1968–1985
94th FIS		Selfridge AFB, Michigan	1960–1969
95th FIS		Dover AFB, Delaware	1959–1973
101st FIS	102nd FIG	Massachusetts ANG	1972–1987
119th FIS	177th FIG	New Jersey ANG	1973–1988
159th FIS	125th FIG	Florida ANG	1974–1986
171st FIS	191st FIG	Michigan ANG	1972–1978
186th FIS	120th FIG	Montana ANG	1972–1987
194th FIS	144th FIW	California ANG	1974–1984
318th FIS	25th AD	McChord AFB, Washington	1959–1983
319th FIS		Malmstrom AFB, Montana	1971–1972
329th FIS		George AFB, California	1960–1967
437th FIS		Oxnard AFB, California	1968–1968
438th FIS		Kincheloe AFB	1960–1968
456th FIS	28th AD	Castle AFB California	1959–1968
460th FIS		Grand Forks AFB, North Dakota	1968–1974
498th FIS	25th AD	Spokane IAP, Washington	1959–1968
539th FIS	26th AD	McGuire AFB, New Jersey	1959–1967

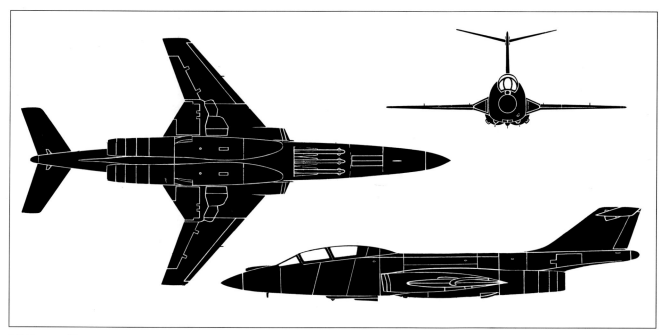

McDonnell F-101 Voodoo

Origin: McDonnell Aircraft Company, St Louis, Missouri
Type: (A, C) day fighter-bomber; (B) all-weather interceptor; (RF) all-weather reconnaissance
Engines: Two Pratt & Whitney J57 two-shaft turbojets with afterburner; (F-101B) 14,990 lb (6800 kg) J57-53 or -55; (others) 14,880 lb (6750 kg) J57-13
Dimensions: Span 39 ft 8 in (12.09 m); length 67 ft 4 ¾ in (20.55 m), (RF) 69 ft 3 in; height 18 ft (34.19 m²)
Weights: Empty (typical of all) 28,000 lb (12,700 kg); maximum loaded (B) 46,700 lb (21,180 kg); (all verslons, overload 51,000 lb (23,133 kg)
Performance: Maximum speed (B) 1220 mph (1963 km/h, Mach 1.85), (others, typical) 1100 mph (1770 km/h); initial climb (B) 17,000 ft (5180 m)/min; service ceiling 52,000 ft (15,850 m); range on internal fuel (B) 1550 miles (2500 km), (others) 1700 miles (2736 km)
Armament: (A) four 20 mm M-39 cannon in nose plus three AIM-4 Falcon AAMs or 12 HVAR rockets on rotary weapon-bay doors; (B) three Falcon (usually AIM-4D) air-to-air missiles semi-recessed in underside, sometimes supplemented by two AIR-2A Genie nuclear rockets on fuselage pylons; (C) three 20 mm M-39 cannon (provision for four, with Tacan removed) in fuselage; (RF) none. As built, all C-models, and derivatives, were fitted with a centreline crutch for a 1 MT tactical nuclear store, and wing pylons for two 2000 lb (907 kg) bombs, four 680 lb (310 kg) mines or other ordnance
History: First flight 29 September 1954; service delivery (A) May 1957; final delivery (B) March 1961

McDonnell Voodoo Operators

2nd FIS	Suffolk County AFB, New York	1959–1969
2nd FITS	ADWC Tyndall AFB, Florida	1974–1982
13th FIS	l9th AD Glasgow AFB, Montana	1959–1968
15th FIS	Davis-Monthan AFB, Arizona	1960–1964
18th FIS	29th AD Grand Forks AFB, North Dakota	1960–1971
29th FIS	Malmstrom AFB, Montana	1960–1968
49th FIS	Griffiths AFB, New York	1959–1968
59th FIS	Kingsley Field, Oregon	1968–1969
60th FIS	Otis AFB, Massachusetts	1959–1971
62nd FIS	30th ADKI Sawyer AFB, Michigan	1959–1971
75th FIS	26th ADDow AFB, Maine	1959–1969
83rd FIS	28th AD Hamilton AFB, California	1960–1963
84th FIS	28th AD Hamilton AFB, California	1959–1968
87th FIS	Lockbourne AFB, Ohio	1960–1968
98th FIS	Dover AFB, Delaware	1959–1968
111th FITS	147th FIG Texas ANG	1971–1975
111th FIS	147th FIG Texas ANG	1976–1982
116th FIS	141st FIG Washington ANG	1969–1976
123rd FIS	142nd FIG Oregon ANG	1971–1982
132nd FIS	101st FIG Maine ANG	1969–1976
136th FIS	170th FIG New York ANG	1971–1982
178th FIS	119th FIG North Dakota ANG	1969–1977
179th FIS	148th FIG Minnesota ANG	1972–1976
322nd FIS	25th AD Kingsley Field, Oregon	1959–1968
437th FIS	Oxnard AFB, California	1960–1968
444th FIS	Charleston AFB, South Carolina	1960–1968
445th FIS	30th AD Wurtsmith AFB, Michigan	1959–1968
No 409 Squadron/CAF	Comox CFB, BC	1962–1985
No 410 Squadron/CAF	Bagotville CFB, Quebec	1961–1982
No 414 Squadron/CAF	North Bay CFB, Ontario	1961–1986
No 416 Squadron/CAF	Chatham CFB, Nova Scotia	1961–1985
No 425 Squadron/CAF	Bagotville CFB, Quebec	1961–1984

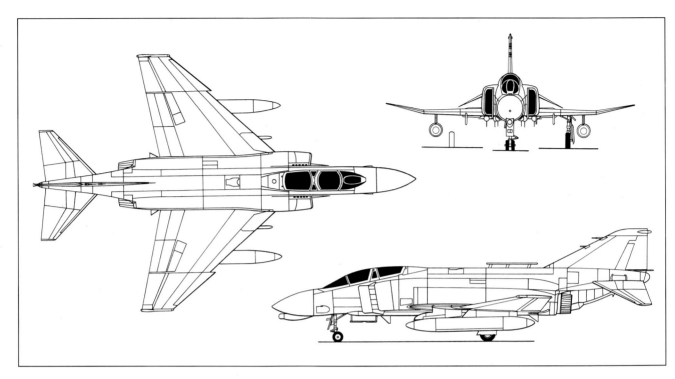

McDonnell Douglas F-4 Phantom II

Origin: McDonnell Aircraft Company, division of McDonnell Douglas, St Louis, Missouri

Type: Originally carrier-based all-weather interceptor, now all-weather multi-role fighter for ship or land operation, RF all-weather multisensor reconnaissance, (QF) RPV, (G) defense-suppression aircraft

Engines: General Electric J79-15 single-shaft turbojets with afterburner (C, D) 17,000 lbs; (E, G) 17,900 lb (8120kg) J79-17

Dimensions: Span 38 ft 5 in (11.7 m); length (C, D,) 58 ft 3 in (17.76 m), (E) 62 ft 11 in or 63 ft (19.2 m); height (all) 16 ft 3 in 4.96 m; wing area 530 sq ft (49.24 m²)

Weights: Empty (C, D) 28,200 lb (12,792 kg), (E) 30,328 lb (13,757 kg), maximum (C, D) 58,000 lb (26,309 kg), (E, G) 60,360 lb (27,379 kg)

Performance: Maximum speed with Sparrow missiles only (low) 910 mph (1464 km/h, Mach 1.19), (high) 1500 mph (2414 km/h, Mach 2.27); initial climb, typically 28,000 ft (8534 m)/min; service ceiling over 60,000 ft (19,685 m); range on internal fuel (no weapons) about 1750 miles (2817 km); ferry range with external fuel, typically 2300 miles (3700 km), (E) 2600 miles (4184 km)

Armament: (All versions except QF, which has no armament) four AIM-7 Sparrow air-to-air missiles recessed under fuselage; inner wing pylons can carry two more AIM-7 or four AIM-9 Sidewinder missiles; in addition all E versions have internal 20 mm M61A1 multi-barrel gun, and virtually all versions can carry the same gun in external centerline pod; all except QF have centerline and four wing pylons for tanks, bombs or other stores to total weight of 16,000 lb (7257 kg)

History: First flight (XF4H-1) 27 May 1958; service delivery (F-4A) February 1960 (carrier trials), February 1961 (inventory); first flight (Air Force F-4C) 27 May 1963, (F-4E) 30 June 1967, (EF-4E, later redesignated F-4G) 1976; final delivery March 1979

ADC Phantom II Users

57th FIS	Air Forces Iceland 1st AF	F-4C	1975 – 1978
57th FIS	Air Forces Iceland	F-4E	1978 – 1985
2nd FWS	325th FWW	F-4C	1977 – 1979
111th FIS	147th FIG Texas ANG	F-4C	1982 – 1987
111th FIS	147th FIG Texas ANG	F-4D	1987 – 1989
123rd FIS	142nd FIG Oregon ANG	F-4C	1982 – 1989
136th FIS	107th FIG New York ANG	F-4C	1982 – 1986
136th FIS	107th FIG New York ANG	F-4D	1986 – 1990
171st FIS	191st FIG Michigan ANG	F-4C	1978 – 1986
171st FIS	191st FIG Michigan ANG	F-4D	1986 – 1990
178th FIS	119th FIG North Dakota ANG	F-4D	1977 – 1990
179th FIS	148th FIG Minnesota ANG	F-4D	1984 – 1990
194th FIS	144th FIG California ANG	F-4D	1984 – 1989

McDonnell Douglas F-15 Eagle

Origin: McDonnell Aircraft Company, St Louis, Missouri
Type: Air superiority fighter with attack capability
Engines: Two 23,930lb (10,855 kg) thrust Pratt & Whitney F100-100 afterburning turbofans
Dimensions: Span 42 ft 9 ¾ in (13.05 m); length 63 ft 9 in (19.43 m); height overall 18 ft 5 ½ in (5.63 m); wing area 608 sq ft (56.5 m²)
Weights: Empty (A) 27,381 lb (12,420 kg); take-off (intercept mission, A) 42,206 lb (19,145 kg); max (A) 56,000 lb (25,401 kg), (C, FAST packs) 68,000 lb (30,845 kg)
Performance: Max speed (clean, over 45,000 ft/13,716 m) 1650 mph (2655 km/h, Mach 2.5), (clean, SL) 912 mph (1468km/h, Mach 1.2); combat ceiling (A, clean) 63,000 ft (19,200 m); time to 50,000 ft (15,240 m) (intercept configuration) 2.5 min; ferry range (C) over 3450 miles (5560km)
Armament: One 20 mm M61A1 gun with 940 rounds; four AIM-7 Sparrow AAMs or eight AIM-120A (AMRAAM), plus four AIM-9 Sidewinders; three attack weapon stations (five with FAST packs) for external load of up to 16,000 1b (7258 kg)
History: First flight 27 July 1972; service delivery (inventory) November 1974; first flight (C) 26 February 1979

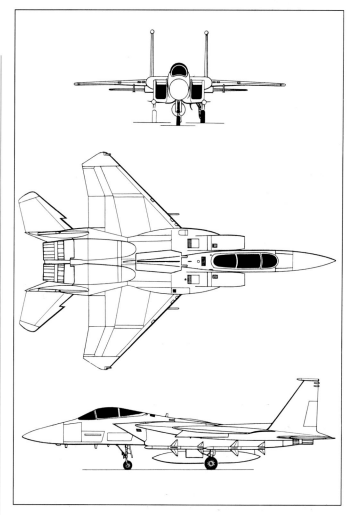

McDonnell Douglas F-15A/D Eagle Units

1st FS	325th FW	Tyndall AFB	1983 – current
2nd FS	325th FW	Tyndall AF	1983 – current
5th FIS	25th AD	Minot AFB	1984 – 1988
7th FS	49th FW	Holloman AFB	1977 – 1991
8th FS	49th FW	Holloman AFB	1977 – 1991
9th FS	49th FW	Holloman AFB	1977 – 1991
12th FS	18th FW	Kadena AFB	1980 – current
22nd FS	36th FW	Bitburg AB	1977 – 1994
22nd FS	48th FW	Lakenheath AB	1994 – current
27th FS	1st FW	Langley AFB	1975 – current
32nd FS	32nd FG	Soesterberg AB	1978 – 1993
43rd FS	21st FW	Elmendorf AFB	1982 – 1991
43rd FS	3rd FW	Elmendorf AFB	1991 – current
44th FS	18th FW	Kadena AFB	1980 – current
48th FIS	23rd AD	Langley AFB	1982 – 1991
53rd FS	36th FW	Bitburg AB	1977 – 1993
53rd FS	52nd FW	Spangdahlem AB	1994 – current
54th FS	21st FW	Elmendorf AFB	1988 – 1991
54th FS	3rd FW	Elmendorf AFB	1991 – current
57th FS	35th FW	NAS Keflavik	1993 – current
57th FS	AFI	NAS Keflavik	1982 – 1993
58th FS	33rd FW	Eglin AFB	1979 – current
59th FS	33rd FW	Eglin AFB	1979 – current
60th FS	33rd FW	Eglin AFB	1981 – current
67th FS	18th FW	Kadena AFB	1980 – current
71st FS	1st FW	Langley AFB	1975 – current
94th FS	1st FW	Langley AFB	1975 – current
95th FS	325th FW	Tyndall AFB	1988 – current
101st FS	103rd FG	Massachusetts ANG	1987 – current
110th FS	132nd FW	Missouri ANG	1991 – current
122nd FS	159th FG	Louisiana ANG	1985 – current
123rd FS	142nd FG	Oregon ANG	1989 – current
128th FS	116th FW	Georgia ANG	1986 – current
199th FS	154th CG	Hawaii ANG	1987 – current
318th FIS	25th AD	McChord AFB	1983 – 1989
390th FS	366th WG	Mountain Home AFB	1992 – current
422nd TES	57th FW	Nellis AFB	1973 – current
426th TFTS	405th TTW	Luke AFB	1981 – 1990
461st TFTS	58th TTW	Luke AFB	1977 – 1979
461st TFTS	405th TTW	Luke AFB	1979 – 1987
525th FS	36th FW	Bitburg AB	1977 – 1991
550th TFTS	58th TTW	Luke AFB	1977 – 1979
550th TFTS	405th TTW	Luke AFB	1979 – 1989
555th TFTS	58th TTW	Luke AFB	1974 – 1979
555th TFTS	405th TTW	Luke AFB	1979 – 1991
4485th TS	AWC	Eglin AFB	1975 – current
6615th TS	6510th TW	Edwards AFB	1974 – current

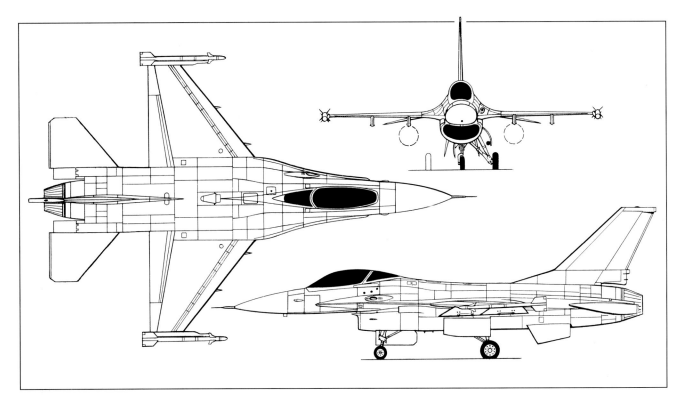

General Dynamics F-16 Fighting Falcon

Origin: General Dynamics; Fort Worth, Texas
Type: (A, ADF, C) Multirole fighter, (B, D) operational
fighter/trainer
Engine: (A, ADF, B, C, D) One 23,840 lb (10,814 kg) thrust Pratt &
Whitney F100-200 afterburning turbofan, (from 1986) 29,000 lb
(13,154 kg) General Electric F110-100 afterburning turbofan
Dimensions: Span 31 ft (9.45 m) (32 ft 10 in/10.1 m over missile
fins); length (all) 49 ft 38 in (15.01 m); height 16 ft 8 ½ in (5.09 m);
wing area 300 sq ft (27.87 m²)
Weights: Empty (A) 16,234 lb (7364 kg), (D) 17,408 lb (7896 kg);
loaded (AMMs only) (A) 23,357 lb (10,594 kg), (B) 22,814 lb (10,348
kg); (max external load) (A, B) 35,400 lb (C, D) 37,500 lb (17,010 kg)
Performance: Max speed (both, AAMs only) 1350 mph (2173 km/h,
Mach 2.05) at 40,000 ft (12.192 m); max at SL 915 mph (1472 km/h,
Mach 1.2); initial climb (AAMs only) 50,000 ft (15,240 m)/min;
service ceiling, over 50,000 ft (15,240 m); tactical radius (A, six Mk 82,
internal fuel, Hi-Lo-Hi) 340 miles (547 km); ferry range 2415 miles
(3890 km)
Armament: One M61A1 20 mm gun with 500/515 rounds; two
AIM-9L/M Sidewinder missiles on wing tip or pylon mounts; two
AMRAAM or AIM-7L Sparrow missiles on underwing pylons;
centreline pylon for 250 gal (1136lit) drop tank of 2200 lb (998 kg)
bomb, inboard wing pylons for 4500 lb (2041 kg) each, middle wing
pylons for 3500 lb (1587 kg) each, outer wing pylons for 700 lb
(318kg) each (being uprated under MSIP-1 to 3500 lb), wingtip
pylons for 425 lb (193 kg), all ratings being at 9g. Normal max load
11,950 lb (5420 kg) for 9g, 20,450 lb (9276 kg) at reduced load factor
History: First flight (YF) 20 January 1974, (production F-16A) 7
August 1978; service delivery (A) 17 August 1978

General Dynamics F-16A ADF Fighting Falcon Units

111th FS	147th FG	Texas ANG	1989 – current
114th FS	142nd FG	Oregon ANG	1988 – current
119th FS	177th FG	New Jersey ANG	1988 – current
134th FS	158th FG	Vermont ANG	1985 – current
136th FS	107th FG	New York ANG	1990 – current
159th FS	125th FG	Florida ANG	1986 – current
169th FS	182nd FG	Illinois ANG	1992 – current
171st FS	191st FG	Michigan ANG	1989 – current
178th FS	119th FG	North Dakota ANG	1989 – current
179th FS	148th FG	Minnesota ANG	1990 – current
186th FS	120th FG	Montana ANG	1987 – current
194th FS	144th FW	California ANG	1989 – current